# WRITING BOOK REVIEWS

# *Writing Book Reviews*

By

JOHN E. DREWRY

Dean, Henry W. Grady School of Journalism, The University of Georgia; Former President, American Association of Teachers of Journalism

GREENWOOD PRESS, PUBLISHERS
WESTPORT, CONNECTICUT

**Library of Congress Cataloging in Publication Data**

Drewry, John Eldridge, 1902-
Writing book reviews.

First published in 1945 under title: Book reviewing.
Reprint of the ed. published by The Writer, inc., Boston.
Bibliography: p.
1. Book reviewing. I. Title.
[PN98.B7D7 1974] 808'.066'0281 73-17951
ISBN 0-8371-7285-3



Originally published in 1966 by The Writer, Inc., Boston

Reprinted with the permission of The Writer, Inc.

Reprinted in 1974 by Greenwood Press, Inc.
51 Riverside Avenue, Westport, CT 06880

Library of Congress catalog card number 73-17951
ISBN 0-8371-7285-3

Printed in the United States of America

10 9 8 7 6 5 4

*The world of books*
*Is the most remarkable creation of man*
*Nothing else that he builds ever lasts*
*Monuments fall*
*Nations perish*
*Civilizations grow old and die out*
*And after an era of darkness*
*New races build others*
*But in the world of books are volumes*
*That have seen this happen again and again*
*And yet live on*
*Still young*
*Still as fresh as the day they were written*
*Still telling men's hearts*
*Of the hearts of men centuries dead*

—Clarence Day

## FOREWORD

IT IS SURPRISING that book reviews and book sections in the average newspaper are so highly valued and yet given so little intelligent attention. Every editor feels, at least vaguely, that he ought to have something in his newspaper about books. He sets aside, perhaps reluctantly, a certain amount of space. Too often neither he nor anyone on his staff has any yardstick with which to measure the real value of such space to his paper. Book reviews are handled in a haphazard fashion, being passed out to reporters or friends of the paper, and the result is about what one would expect. (I am speaking, of course, of the average newspaper and not of those few which do a superlative job.)

Now comes John E. Drewry, Dean of the Henry W. Grady School of Journalism of the University of Georgia, with the first clear, practical, and common-sense guide for anyone who wishes to review books. It has the added virtue of being intelligently and pleasingly written. Dean Drewry has for a good many years conducted a book review column, which has been a popular feature in Southern newspapers. In addition, he has made this phase of journalistic instruction one which received emphasis in his school.

It seems to me this book would be of interest and value to the average reader in that it would teach him better how to read a book. Also, for those editors who have no trained book reviewer, I can recommend they take a copy of this book and give it to the person assigned to the book review sections and say, "Study this." It is a recommendation I expect to take myself. I think, too, it merits a place in the study course of each school of journalism.

—Ralph McGill, Publisher
*The Atlanta Constitution*

# PREFACE

This is a completely revised version of an earlier book titled *Book Reviewing,* first published in 1945 and reprinted in 1946. All of the material in the original book has been brought up to date and much material has been added.

As explained in the Preface of the original edition, I have since the early 1920's written a column, "New Book News," which has been used by the *Athens Banner-Herald, Atlanta Journal, Atlanta Constitution, Savannah Evening Press,* and other newspapers. I have also done reviews for *Publishers' Auxiliary* and other specialized publications. During this period I have at various times, in connection with my duties as dean of the University of Georgia's Henry W. Grady School of Journalism, taught a course in book reviewing. Some years ago, it was my privilege to study at Columbia University under the late Allen Sinclair Will, night city editor of the *New York Times* and a regular contributor of full-length feature reviews to the Sunday *Times* Book Review. For more than four decades, I have read widely and observed closely the practices of the best media of literary criticism.

This book, therefore, is the result of all this experience, instruction, and reading. It was first suggested by Dr. Edd Winfield Parks, a member of our English faculty, whose implication, I assumed, was that one who had been as close to book reviewing as long as I have must have a few helpful suggestions worth passing along to others.

Like the college courses in musical and literary appreciation, this book is intended for several groups; not only for practitioners, actual and would-be, but also for those who read merely for enjoyment. In a sense, this may be regarded as a guide to intelligent comprehension as well as to competent reviewing.

Almost everyone has to prepare a book report of some kind at some time. In every grade and type of grammar, high school, preparatory, college, and university course, preparation of reading reports is a part of the academic procedure. This little book should be not without value in this connection.

In the preparation of the first edition of *Book Reviewing*, I was aided by Hoyt N. Ware, U. S. Information Service, Embassy of the United States of America, Panama, and previously with the *Savannah Press* and the Associated Press. In this revision, I have been assisted by two members of our School of Journalism staff, Mrs. Tyus Butler and George Watts. To these, my thanks. To A. S. Burack, editor of The Writer, Inc., a special word of appreciation for his interest and help with this book, going back to the time of the first edition.

J. E. D.

Henry W. Grady School of Journalism
The University of Georgia, Athens

## CONTENTS

*Criticism is neither the scales that weigh nor the icing that sweetens, but the yeast that, for readers, leavens the lump. A good reviewer must have cool brains and a warm heart. He must have enthusiasms and guard them, and his likings must be as strong as his hates.*

—Henry Seidel Canby.

## ACKNOWLEDGMENTS

Grateful acknowledgment is hereby extended to those individuals, periodicals, and publishers to whom the writer is indebted for quotations and ideas.

In the case of quotations, credit and permissions to reprint are noted in the proper places on subsequent pages.

As for ideas, these are a bit more difficult to pin down. Nonetheless, every effort has been made to acknowledge all known sources, and appreciation is here expressed to all who have contributed to the writer's views on the subject of this book.

The author is especially indebted to those "experts" whose words of wisdom about reviewing are quoted and examples of whose work are reproduced. To them and to the publications in which their utterances and/or reviews first appeared, our thanks.

As for the brief quotations at the beginnings of chapters, some of these are from material on which the copyright has long since expired and others are by living persons. To both groups, the publisher and author are appreciative of the privilege of quoting these pertinent gems.

# I

# THE KEY TO THIS BOOK

*Books are keys to wisdom's treasure;*
*Books are gates to lands of pleasure;*
*Books are paths that upward lead;*
*Books are friends. Come, let us read.*

—Inscription for the Children's Reading
Room, Hopkinton, Massachusetts

## THE KEY TO THIS BOOK

A BOOK REVIEW is essentially the answer to certain very ordinary questions that occur to one as a new (or old) book is discussed—

Who wrote the book?

What is it about?

How does it compare with other books by the same author?

How does it compare with other books on the same subject or in the same field?

And other simple questions of a similar character.

Book reviews may be—

*Written* (for newspapers, magazines, trade publications, or as school assignments, etc.);

*Spoken* (as broadcast or televised, or read at lectures or club meetings, etc.); or

*Silent* (as one, in his own thinking, mulls over, analyzes, and evaluates some book he has read).

Which means that book reviewing can be a vocation, an avocation, or simply a form of literary appreciation, as personal and private as enjoying good music or the stage.

Or, it may be a form of stern, scientific mental discipline. The story is told of a psychology professor who wrote a review of every book he read, only to throw each review immediately in the wastebasket. Not that they were not worth publishing. Some were. But that was not their primary purpose. Good psychologist that he was, he knew that one remembers best those things to which he has actively reacted. When one thinks enough about a book to do a review—with all that the review implies—he is making that book a part of him—his thinking and memory processes.

All of which is said by way of stating the key to this volume.

The key?

Questions and answers.

This book provides the questions, and you, as you read, will furnish the answers.

For each of the major classes of books—biography, history, etc.—you will find in subsequent pages a list of a dozen or more questions. Write down the answers to these after you have read a book, and you will have the raw material of your review.

Some of the questions will yield only a single sentence by way of reply. Others will give you many sentences—a paragraph, or more. Rearrangement of the answers to these questions—selection of your lead, general theme, choice of material for quotation purposes, etc.—will provide, in essence, your review. It is as simple as that.

What are these questions? Here they are—

But first, a few simple definitions and general observations, with a word or so from some of our leading contemporary book reviewers.

# II

# WHAT IS A BOOK REVIEW?

*There's no book so bad but something good may be found in it.*

*He that publishes a book runs a very great hazard, since nothing can be more impossible than to compose one that may secure the approbation of every reader.*

—Miguel de Cervantes.

*A bad book is as much of a labour to write as a good one; it comes as sincerely from the author's soul.*

—Aldous Huxley.

## WHAT IS A BOOK REVIEW?

MOST BOOK REVIEWS are either an objective or a subjective essay about some particular book, usually of recent publication.

In the objective review, the emphasis is on the book and its author—the aim, plan, and scope of the book, and the special qualifications of the writer in terms of this particular book.

In the subjective review, the emphasis is on the reviewer—his reaction to and evaluation of the book; what he thinks about the subject; and what he knows on this theme which the author may or may not have included, intentionally or unintentionally.

Harry Hansen, long-time reviewer for the New York *World-Telegram, Harper's, Redbook,* etc., may be cited as a good example of the objective type of reviewer. Edmund Wilson's articles on books, like most of his writing, tend to be subjective. Clifton Fadiman has something of both. His reviews give a good picture of the books under discussion, but they also reflect his personality.

Book reviews may also be thought of as judicial or impressionistic.

In the judicial review, a book is described and evaluated in terms of accepted literary and historical standards. The review is really a criticism—the scholarly appraisal of a student of a particular subject, period, or author.

In the impressionistic review, a book is interpreted against a background of the author's avowed purposes and a common-sense estimate as to whether these have been achieved. This kind of review is primarily a job in reporting—exposition of the aim of a book and author, and how well this has been realized.

The scholarly, technical, and professional periodicals, making a specialized appeal and entrusting their reviews to experts, are most interested in judicial reviews. Newspapers, popular magazines, and radio-TV, on the other hand, making a mass appeal, are the media of impressionistic reviews.

The judicial review is sometimes referred to as the critique, which may be defined as a scholarly essay about a book or an author, or about several, written by a person of erudition and specialized knowledge, appealing primarily to a limited but learned group—the appeal being restricted because the article is devoted largely to finely spun academic questions.

"True literary criticism," says Clifton Fadiman, "is a subtle and venerable art. You can number the top-notchers on your fingers and toes: Aristotle, Horace, Coleridge, Lessing, Sainte-Beuve, Taine, Goethe, Arnold, Shaw (one of the greatest), and a few others. In our time and nation, literary criticism is almost a lost art, partly because no one except for a few other literary critics cares to read it." *

In like fashion, the impressionistic review is also known as the descriptive review, and may be defined as that prose form in which the writer, without over-enthusiasm or exaggeration, gives the essential information about a book. This he does by description and exposition, by quoting striking

* From *Reading I've Liked,* edited by Clifton Fadiman, Simon and Schuster, Inc.

passages—especially if they are indicative of the author's style and manner, and by an indirect evaluation, usually in terms of the author's aims and purposes.

The ideal review has qualities of both the judicial-critique and the impressionistic-descriptive review. It is essentially an exercise in objective expository writing. All of which boils down to this: the difference between the review and criticism, a difference which has been explained admirably by Llewellyn Jones:*

"The difference between criticizing a book and reviewing it may be stated very simply. If you read a book and write a summary of its contents, telling the ground it covers, possibly noting the style, you have written a review of the book. You have, that is, informed the possible reader as to what is in the book. *You have done a job of reporting. And like the reporter you have kept yourself out of the story.* If, on the other hand, you talk about the book in terms of your own point of view, if you say whether you think the book is a good one or a bad one, giving your reasons for so stating, you are writing criticism. . . .

"Most people think of a book as a thing in itself. They tell their younger friends that they must not bury themselves in books 'for life is more important than books'. They refer to people who prefer books to jazz as 'bookworms'. But there is no such thing as a *book* in and for itself. The word *book* comes from the same Indo-European root as the word *box,* and this accident of heredity is suggestive. A book is no more than a box—as we may readily see by examining a specimen of each. The box has a cover and so has the book, and the

* From *How to Criticize Books,* by Llewellyn Jones, W. W. Norton and Company, Inc.

box has contents and so has the book—and then again both may be empty. If you knew an African explorer who kept a lot of boxes for packing his trophies, you would never think of saying that Mr. Smith is a very boxish man. And by the same token you should never refer to a person who is fond of reading as a bookish man. If he reads more than you do the chances are that he knows more about life than you do."

Macmillan's well-known editor Harold S. Latham adds, "Now reviewers have a function—don't misunderstand me! They do and should play an important part in the book world, but I think that part should be more informative than critical. If the reader is told the nature of a volume and its general theme and purpose, he will have a basis for deciding whether it is something he wishes to read or not. Too often the professional critic lets his prejudices color his conclusions. By making clear what a given volume is all about and allowing the reader to select or discard as he sees fit, the critic would be performing a service to the average reader. This is the principle I have followed in selecting the books I have wished to read; if the subject matter appealed to me, I secured the book and on reading it formed my own judgment as to its literary worth. In many cases I would have missed out on books that had real value for me if I had been guided solely by the critics' evaluations. What I have proposed would, it seems to me, be fairer to author and reader than the present practices frequently are. It would permit the one to have an unprejudiced public and the other to read a work in which he might be considerably interested but from which he would have been put off by a biased reviewer." *

* From *My Life in Publishing,* by Harold S. Latham, E. P. Dutton.

The book review, insofar as journalism is concerned, has characteristics of the news story, the editorial, and the special feature article.

It is like the news story, as Mr. Jones' quotation indicates, because it portrays the contents of a book just as other stories describe fires, accidents, and other items in the news.

The review is like the editorial in that it is interpretative and explanatory. It reveals the opinion and critical evaluation of the writer, although, as said before, this should be indirect and held to a minimum in the objective-descriptive review.

The review is not only like the feature article, but in many instances *is* a special feature. Willard G. Bleyer has defined the feature article as "a detailed presentation of facts in an interesting form adapted to rapid reading, for the purpose of entertaining or informing the average person." This definition applies equally well to the book review, and suggests a fundamental point about the review, viz., it should be an article worth reading in itself, regardless of whether one has read or plans to read the book about which it is written.

The foregoing statement suggests another question:

Who reads book reviews, and why?

There are several groups:

1. Those who use reviews as guides to their book choices.

2. Those who, having read a book, are interested in seeing what others have to say about it.

3. Those who do not have the time to read books and who must therefore rely on reviews for their information about the news of the literary world.

4. Those who read a review in the same way that they would an editorial, a political article, or a Walter Winchell

column. They are reading their newspaper and magazine and are attracted to anything that looks interesting.

If a reviewer can satisfy groups three and four, the first two will probably also be pleased. In order to meet the requirements of groups three and four, there are certain minimum essentials which the review should accomplish. They are:

1. A description of the book.

2. Something about the author.

3. A comparison of the book to others by the same author and in the same field.

4. An appraisal, preferably indirect, through description and exposition in terms of the aims and purposes of the author.

Dr. Allan Nevins has very wisely observed that "criticism is implicit in any good summary or exposition. . . . The very arrangement of your exposition, the way in which you emphasize some parts of a book and ignore other parts, is a form of criticism. . . ."

A review which possesses these basic essentials and which is written with verve and gusto is quite likely to be an interesting article in itself, well worth reading independently of the book upon which it is based.

# III

# BACKGROUND FOR REVIEWING

*All the world knows me in my book, and my book in me.*

—Michel de Montaigne.

*A man will turn over half a library to make one book.*

—Samuel Johnson.

## BACKGROUND FOR REVIEWING

THE PERSON WHO intends to review books, either as a vocation or in connection with other literary, journalistic, or professional work, should feel at home among books—other than textbooks.

He should be curious about all phases of the book world —how books come to be published, how they are distributed and sold after they have been printed, the work of the literary agent, publicity and promotion, jackets and illustrations, and numerous other similar aspects of the business of books.

"Bring into a room two statesmen," writes Earl Schenck Miers, "and very likely you will have a war, two churchmen and you will have a schism, two businessmen and you will have a merger or a panic, two murderers and you will have a murder, but bring into the same room two men who work and live with books and the walls will ring with camaraderie." *

The reviewer should know his way around in libraries, large and small, college and municipal, public and private. He should not only know his way about, but he should have that affection for books and authors which makes him delight in browsing.

"Why is there no other genteel vice quite to compare with the leisurely indulgence of book browsing?" asks Mr. Miers.

* From *Bookmaking and Kindred Amenities,* edited by Earl Schenck Miers and Richard Ellis, Rutgers University Press.

"Why does the very touch of a fine book exhilarate the body and leave a glow in eyes and cheeks and heart? A good part of the answer, I suspect, lies in the creative impulse which gives birth to each of these moments, an impulse that is the living soul of everything which on this earth strives to establish kinship with eternity. A book is a monument to a man, in a very real sense his embodiment, for it is wrung from his sweat and tears, and impelled by the seed of his intellect."

For those who wish to become more than merely good craftsmen in reviewing, one thing in particular is to be stressed: *the more one brings to the task of reading and reviewing by way of personal erudition, understanding, and discrimination, the better job he can do.* A review, just as other forms of prose writing, reflects the quality of mind of the one who writes it. If this be of a high order, the review is likely to be an essay on the same level. If not, the review will be correspondingly mediocre. This means that the master reviewer brings to each book not only some knowledge of the field represented by the book, but a good cultural background—the sort of education and sensitivity which the liberal arts college, at its best, imparts. In the language of Dr. John Donald Wade, editor of *Masterworks of World Literature,* etc., "the more the reviewer himself, personally, knows, thinks, feels, is, etc., the more, naturally, he will have to convey to his followers."

There are certain subjects and materials with which the reviewer should be acquainted, and which he should examine with some regularity. These would include:

1. *The better book review pages and sections of representative American newspapers (and of certain foreign newspapers).*

Among these would be the daily book page and Sunday Book Review section of the New York *Times* and New York *Herald Tribune* (the *Tribune's* section, called *Book Week*, is also included in the Washington *Post* and Chicago *Sun-Times*), the Chicago *Tribune, Christian Science Monitor*, and other papers of similar size and prestige, as well as the London *Times Literary Supplement, The Observer, The Spectator, The New Statesman, Le Monde, Le Figaro, L'Express*, etc.

The reviewer should note in particular the review columns and pages in his own locality. Some of these are quite distinctive and good.

2. *The book sections of certain weekly and monthly publications.*

Foremost among these would be *Harper's Magazine*, the *Atlantic Monthly* (with "The Peripatetic Reviewer" by the editor Edward Weeks), *The New York Review of Books, The New Yorker, The Saturday Review, Time, Newsweek, Life, The Reporter, The Commonweal, The New Republic* and *The Nation*. Also important would be such magazines as *Commentary, The Partisan Review, The Sewanee Review, The Kenyon Review, The Virginia Quarterly Review*, etc.

3. *Radio and television programs devoted to books and authors.*

Individual radio and television stations and networks are giving increasingly more attention to books and authors. Regular comments on and reviews of new books, interviews with authors of popular best sellers, and other literary features are being used as sustaining and commercial programs. These range from "The Readers' Almanac" conducted by Warren Bower (on WNYC, New York, picked up by the

Voice of America and re-broadcast over NAEB Tape Network) to "Carnival of Books," a children's book and author series carried by stations across the country.

As he reads book columns and pages, or as he listens to radio or television programs of a literary nature, the reviewer should have something of the critical or analytical attitude. Points which he may notice, formally or informally, depending upon the extent of his interest, are (1) size and format; (2) frequency and time of issue; (3) scope, including books listed as well as reviewed; (4) length of reviews; (5) point of view of reviewer—that is, descriptive or critical; (6) personnel and qualifications of reviewers; (7) advertising—quantity, position, etc.; and (8) illustrations.

In an analysis of an individual review, attention should be given to structure, style, lead, adequacy of description, critical evaluation, reviewer's qualifications and attitude, length, etc.

4. *Publicity material of the various publishing houses.*

In addition to their commercial advertising, most of the larger publishing houses and some of the university presses issue regular newsletters and other publicity matter. Announcements of forthcoming books, news notes about authors and their whereabouts and activities, human interest stories and feature articles about the men and women back of current best sellers, digests of the critical comment on various books, photographs of authors, and similar items are included in these publicity services. Their value to one who conducts a book page, or writes a regular column, or who does reviews will be readily appreciated. These publicity letters are in a sense the literary editor's equivalent of the Associated Press or United Press International service for a newspaper's telegraph editor. They are a major contact with the centers of book publishing. They keep him in touch with what publishers are planning and doing; what authors are lecturing where, and why; which biographer is seeking data on this or that worthy; and a multitude of related topics. They provide valuable background and atmosphere.

5. *Literary agents and their work.*

Literature has produced its own species of entrepreneur—a kind of middleman between author and publisher, a salesman of articles, stories, and books, who makes the contacts for a writer with magazine editors, book publishers, motion picture and stage producers, and television executives. He receives a commission on the author's payment or royalty, and it is to his advantage, therefore, to market an author's work as profitably as possible. The better literary agents limit their clientele to the established, successful writers.

6. *Publishing vs. printing, including "vanity publishers."*

Printing is just one phase of publishing. When one has a commercial printer print a manuscript, he has done but one of the steps that concern the broad domain of publishing. Book publishing is a huge enterprise which involves examination and selection of manuscripts, assigning subjects for prospective books to qualified writers, editing, designing of formats, proofreading, preparation of dummies for salesmen on the road, planning of advertising, publicity and promotion, distribution of review copies, collections, bookkeeping, payment of royalties to author, and other such things. Among several invaluable publications giving information on publishing, bookselling, reviewing, etc., are two issued by the R. R. Bowker Company: *Publishers' Weekly,* a trade magazine, and *Literary Market Place,* a business directory of American book publishing issued annually and available at most libraries.

Most books are published on a royalty basis, i.e., the publisher assumes full financial responsibility for the production and distribution of the volume, and the author is paid a percentage of the gross receipts. The percentage is usually ten per cent on the first edition and higher on subsequent printings. Books of a scholarly nature, restricted in appeal, are sometimes subsidized, wholly or in part, by the author or by some foundation or association interested in their publication. Such volumes are to be distinguished clearly from those privately printed by an author. In the case of the published book, the volume has the prestige of the publisher's imprint and the benefit of his editorial and other publishing services. The privately printed book usually reflects the absence of the guiding hand of an experienced publisher.

"Vanity publisher" is a term applied to a firm of questionable character which "publishes" (usually only prints, because its distribution facilities are limited) the work of a novitiate—a work which has generally been rejected by one or more reputable publishers—in exchange for a financial consideration. The "consideration" is often exorbitant and the whole procedure is one to be avoided. If a work is worth publishing, it can be done in some other more sensible fashion. *Mail Fraud,* a pamphlet obtainable from the Chief Postal Inspector, U. S. Post Office Dept., Washington, D. C. 20260, comments, "A genuine publisher will tell you the truth about the value of your writing and will assume all costs for publishing your work. Legitimate publishers never charge a fee in connection with publishing and you should suspect anyone who offers any such proposition."

7. *How to secure review copies.*

There are two approaches to this topic: (1) that of the individual, and (2) that of a publication.

In the first case, a person desiring to do reviews should arrange an introduction, in person or by letter, with the particular editor of the newspaper or periodical who is responsible for the book section. Most book editors have a list of regular reviewers upon whom they rely for the bulk of their reviews. These consist of staff members, local persons known for their ability as writers, and specialists in various fields. A newcomer who offers promise, however, is usually welcome, and the book editor is ordinarily willing to give him a trial with some book of lesser importance. If his review of this meets the requirements of the editor, he will probably be given other books and, in time, may have his name added to the list of regular reviewers for the publication. Such free-lance or contributing reviewers are paid on a space-rate basis, a flat sum for each review, or are given the book in exchange for the review, depending on the size and policy of the publication.

In securing review copies directly from a publisher, the approach ordinarily is made by the newspaper or magazine, through the editor responsible for the book section. Publishers set aside a certain number of copies of each new title for editorial purposes. Some of these go to certain mailing lists, such as the book editors of leading newspapers, book editors of various magazines, book editors of press associations and syndicates, editors of specialized periodicals (for certain types of books), etc. Others are used to fill special requests. The representative of a newspaper or other publication, in requesting a review copy, should give the essential information about his medium, i.e., its circulation, the population of the community in which it is published, any distinctive characteristics of the publication or the town, etc. Clippings of all reviews should be sent to the publishers of the respective books. These may be mailed as they appear (many newspapers have the various publishing houses on their mailing lists for the book page), or they may be sent in along with requests for other titles from a given publishing house. If the latter plan is followed, the reviews should be filed by publisher as they appear. Then when the reviewer next requests a title from a particular firm, he will have readily available clippings of recent reviews of other titles bearing this imprint. Such a plan keeps the reviewer in touch with publishers and incidentally is indicative of his good faith. This is said because publishers receive many requests for review copies from persons who are simply seeking free books and who have no intention or means of giving them adequate notice.

# IV

# THE TECHNIQUE OF REVIEWING

*Go forth, my book, and take whatever pounding*
*The heavy fisted destinies prepare.*
*I know you are not anything astounding,*
*And, to be quite sincere, I don't much care.*
*Get off your overcoat, the gong is sounding.*
*The enemy has risen from his chair.*
*He doesn't look so overwhelming, but*
*His arm is long. Watch for an uppercut.*

—Leonard Bacon.

*As good almost kill a man as kill a good book: who kills a man kills a reasonable creature, God's image; but he who destroys a good book kills reason itself. . . .*

—John Milton.

## THE TECHNIQUE OF REVIEWING

THE TECHNIQUE of book reviewing is much simpler than such an academic term as technique would seem to imply. It involves a few obvious steps such as—

1. Choosing a book.

2. Reading the book.

3. Making some notes about the book, mentally or, better, on paper.

4. Analyzing the medium (newspaper, magazine, trade journal, radio or television program, etc.) in which the review is to be used.

5. Mulling over, as one goes about his regular work (reporting, teaching, preaching, studying, cooking, looking after the children, etc.), the content of the book in an effort to arrive at an appropriate theme, or angle, or peg, for the review.

6. Organization of the notes, mentioned under No. 3, into a suitable outline—a structure which will harmonize with and incorporate the theme decided upon under No. 5.

7. The writing of the review.

8. Editing and revision of the manuscript.

9. Recopying and preparation of final draft.

10. Publication or broadcast of the review.

In the selection of a book for review, one should choose within subjects about which he has background. The more he reads, the wider will become his intellectual horizon and the greater will be the range of titles from which he may select. Clifton Fadiman says that he tries "to juggle five factors, whose relative importance varies with each book": (1) his personal interest in a book ("I am apt to write more usefully about something that engages my attention. I don't have to like the book necessarily. It may interest me because its author happens to represent a great many things I dislike . . ."); (2) the news value of the book; (3) the appeal of the volume to readers of a particular publication; (4) the opinion of a publisher as to the importance of a volume ("If a publisher writes me that Hyacinthe Doakes' novel is terrific, that he is going to lay ten thousand dollars' worth of advertising money on the line—why, I make a note to read Hyacinthe's book with care. I may not like it, and in that case will say so. But . . . I am more apt to like it than some little yarn this same publisher . . . hides away in the back of his catalogue. Publishers . . . know a good deal about books and their judgment of the relative values of their productions is hearkened to by any sensible reviewer."); and (5) the intrinsic significance of the work itself.*

As for reading and making notes on the book, different types of books can be read with varying degrees of speed. Mr. Fadiman said in this connection: ". . . I do not believe dogmatically either in fast or slow reading. I believe tripe should be read practically with the speed of light and, let us say, Toynbee's *A Study of History,* with tortoise deliberation. And most books are nearer to tripe than to Toynbee. . . . Most of us . . . suffer from chronic reverence. We make an unwarranted assumption that because a man is in

* From *Reading I've Liked,* edited by Clifton Fadiman, Simon and Schuster, Inc.

print he has something to say, and, acting on this assumption, we read his every word with scrupulous care. This may be good manners but it's a confounded waste of time."

Speed in reading, wrote Lewis Gannett of the New York *Herald Tribune,* is "largely a matter of attention. The lay reader is likely to think of reading in terms of the relaxed hour before he goes to sleep. The professional critic reads as if he were cramming for an examination every day, and he gets through fast. I think of it in terms of gear-shift. I discovered long ago that it takes me longer to read a book in the country than in tense New York. But in city or country, I start reading any book in low gear. I begin slowly; I make copious notes; I browse my way into the author's mood and cast of characters. . . . Long books I sometimes read by the clock. If I am not making my minimum hundred pages an hour—or more, depending on the type of book—I must force myself to a more energetic pace. It is exhausting, but it can be done."

As one reads a book for review, he should mark, possibly with a perpendicular line in the margin (if the book be his own), those passages which are in the nature of key utterances—topics for his outline, or which are so well phrased or so typical of an author's style and manner that they seem especially suited for direct quotation.

Edward Weeks, editor of *The Atlantic Monthly,* has suggested that "as you read, try to keep one portion of your mind somewhat detached from the main current of the narrative itself. Once you have learned to cultivate this detachment you will be impelled to pause every now and then to make note of certain pros and cons in the book. Suppose a character seems to you too flat to be serviceable, suppose an episode seems to you too incredible to be believed in, then you had better make note of your impression before it is effaced. I have found that the blank white leaves provide me with a convenient closet for these odds and ends of criticism. I jot them down as hastily as possible in shortcut English of my own, and when the book is done and it is time to assimilate my impressions I turn to this 'closet' and find what I need."

Analyzing the medium will prove valuable because such an examination will aid the reviewer with the style and structure of his review. He will see the kind of thing the publication prefers, and can plan his article accordingly. Some points to note in medium analysis are to be found in the chapter on "Background for Reviewing."

As for mulling over one's review before it is written, the word *mull* means, according to the dictionary, to work mentally, to cogitate, to ponder, to ruminate. And that is just exactly what a reviewer should do—for quite a period. There should be an interval set aside for this purpose between reading the book and writing the review.

An outline or skeleton of the review is a guide to orderly, coherent, effective writing. "It may seem a useless bit of trouble to outline anything so brief," writes Dr. Allan Nevins, "but it is not. In the end, the outline of any written work, even of a social letter, will reduce the labor involved, and at the same time greatly improve the product."

As one considers steps 7 and 8, writing and editing the review, he should remember that one is essentially a creative endeavor, while the other is a task in correction. One is a job of production, while the other is an assignment in inspection. One calls for the enthusiasm and zeal of the doer, while the other demands the calm caution and the steady hand of the surgeon. The two tasks involve separate and distinct mental and emotional processes. They should not be done at the same time. One should not interfere with the normal flow of his ideas, facts, and language while he is writing to stop and edit. Complete the writing, get the ideas on paper, and then come back later and check on spelling, punctuation, and other items of style, grammar, and rhetoric.

Dorothea Brande in her *Becoming a Writer* (Harcourt, Brace) develops this idea at some length by pointing out that there are basically two sides to a writer's emotional and spiritual makeup—the craftsman and the critic. "When the actual writing is to be done," she says, "your elder self must stand aside, only murmuring a suggestion now and again on such matters as your tendency to use repetitions, or to suggest that you are being too verbose, or that the dialogue is getting out of hand. Later you will call on it to consider the completed draft, or section, and with its help you will alter the manuscript to get the best possible effects. But at the time of writing, nothing is more confusing than to have the alert, critical, overscrupulous rational faculty at the forefront of your mind. The tormenting doubts of one's own ability, the self-conscious muteness that drops like a pall over the best story-ideas, come from consulting the judge in oneself at the moment when it is the story teller's turn to be in the ascendant. It is not easy at first to inhibit the running verdicts on every sentence, almost every word, that is written, but once the flow of the story has well set in, the critical faculty will be content to wait its turn."

As one makes the final copy of his review, he should note such small things as the indicia, i.e., the exact title, the complete name and address of the publisher, etc. In many publications, this general information is compressed into a statistical paragraph, usually in the form of a series of short phrases that should contain, in order, the title of the book, author's name, city where published, name of publisher, number of pages (abbreviated), and price, thus:

> THE SOURCE. By James A. Michener. New York: Random House. 909 pp. $7.95.

There are several variations in the use of indicia. Some reviewers, notably those who write for the New York *Times Book Review,* list the indicia at the beginning of the review. Others list the indicia at the end of the review. In *Saturday Review,* information about the reviewer is often included along with indicia.

The reviewer should keep a copy of his review, for various reasons, one of which is that in this way he can compare the printed version with his original and thereby note editorial changes, some of which may have meaning and will serve as guides in his future work.

# V

# BIOGRAPHY

*The history of the world is but the biography of great men.*

—Thomas Carlyle.

*There is properly no History; only Biography.*

—Ralph Waldo Emerson.

*A man who leaves memoirs, whether well or badly written, provided they be sincere, renders a service to future psychologists and writers.*

—Henryk Sienkiewicz.

## BIOGRAPHY

CATHERINE DRINKER BOWEN, in her excellent book *The Writing of Biography,* writes, "Somebody asked Charles Dickens about his rules of composition, the artistic principles by which he proceeded. 'I have only one artistic principle,' he said. 'That is, to rouse the emotions of my readers.' Between novelist and biographer the difference is profound. The one invents situations that will rouse a reader's emotions; the other brings out the significance of situations that already exist. Both are concerned with *la recherche du temps perdu,* both wish to uncover the nature or motivation of man."

If one would understand human nature—the hopes and aspirations, the achievements and failures, the guiding philosophies of the great and near-great—there is no better way than to turn to some of the many autobiographies and biographies which today rival fiction in their appeal.

This increasing interest in biography would seem to indicate that the complexities of modern civilization are making more and more people conscious of what they may learn from those who have enjoyed full, rich lives.

"To study others, to know others, even in the very moderate degree in which it is possible, helps us to put ourselves in others' places and to put others in ours, and the outcome of such knowledge must necessarily be at least some increase in patience, in sympathy, in tolerance, in love."

So wrote Gamaliel Bradford, for years America's preeminent biographer, in his illuminating *Biography and the Human Heart*. Bradford is the writer who introduced the term *psychography,* and who, along with Lytton Strachey, is credited with influencing much twentieth century biographical writing.

Psychography, according to Mr. Bradford, "is the attempt to portray character, and in discussing psychography, we must . . . begin with a clear understanding of what character means. . . . Character is quite distinct from individuality. . . . Character . . . is the sum of qualities of generalized habits of action. Psychography is the condensed, essential, artistic presentation of character. . . . Out of the perpetual flux of actions and circumstances that constitutes a man's whole life, it seeks to extract what is essential, what is permanent, and (what is) vitally characteristic."

This reference to psychography suggests other terminology, peculiar to this field, with which the reviewer should be familiar—such terms as the following:

*Autobiography*—biography written by the subject himself or herself. Dr. Joseph Collins (*The Doctor Looks at Biography*) says that "the main difference between autobiography and biography . . . is that the former works from within outwards, while the latter works from without inwards; and the autobiographer is successful only in proportion to the self-absorption he reveals; his is a selfish and personal work. The biographer, on the other hand, is successful only in proportion to the self-effacement he shows."

There are critical arguments for and against autobiography. André Maurois* maintains that "there are several causes which tend to make an autobiographical narrative in-

* In *Aspects of Biography,* Frederick Ungar Pub. Co.

accurate and false," including ". . . the fact that we forget . . . deliberate forgetfulness on aesthetic grounds . . . that perfectly natural censorship which the mind exercises upon whatever is disagreeable . . . (that) form of censorship . . . which is operated by a sense of shame . . . memory not only fails . . . but, above all, it rationalizes . . . (and) the perfectly legitimate device to protect those who have been our companions in the actions which we describe."

Dr. Samuel Johnson on the other hand, maintained that "every man's life should be best written by himself."

*Letters and diaries*—a form of autobiography, often chatty, informal, and trivial, but sometimes of major historical and literary significance, as in the case of *Journal of a Soul* by Pope John XXIII, *Markings* by Dag Hammarskjöld, or the many multi-volume editions of the letters and papers of our early Presidents that are now being issued.

*Authorized biography*—a term applied to a life-story written at the behest of or by permission of the subject, his family, or his literary legatees. This form has obvious advantages and disadvantages. On the positive side, the authorized biographer has ready access to personal correspondence, intimate papers, and other valuable original source material. On the negative side, a subject or his family may sometimes try, consciously or unconsciously, deliberately or indirectly, to shape the tone, spirit, or quality of the resulting narrative.

Something of the inherent weakness of authorized biography is revealed in the following extract by Mr. Strachey: ". . . Those two fat volumes, with which it is our custom to commemorate the dead—who does not know them, with their ill-digested masses of material, their slipshod style, their tone of tedious panegyric, their lamentable lack of selection, of detachment, of design? They are as familiar as the cortege of the undertaker, and wear the same air of slow, funereal barbarism."

*Campaign biography*—the life-story with a purpose, usually political. Such biographies are often hastily prepared for free distribution, and in many instances are superficial and one-sided. Campaign biographies vary, of course, in quality, and some possess a high degree of truthfulness and readability.

*Debunking biography*—a term which came into being during the 1920's when H. L. Mencken and his *American Mercury* were riding the crest of the wave of post-war cynicism and criticism—the era of such books as W. E. Woodward's *George Washington: The Image and the Man* and *Meet General Grant*. To Lytton Strachey belongs much of the credit—if credit be the word—for popularizing this form of biographical writing. "His precise ironic style and the severity of his attitude did much to introduce the depreciatory biographies of the post-war period." So reads a part of his sketch in *The Concise Oxford Dictionary of English Literature*. There are, of course, many satellites, too numerous to mention, whose glow of varying degrees of intensity has helped illumine the biographical skies during the past twenty-odd years.

*Fictionized biography*—a cross between novel and formal biography, which features the romance, drama, suspense, and climax of the first, and the fact of the second. Illustrative of this type of life study are such popular works as *Ariel* by André Maurois* *Thomas* by Shelley Mydans, and *The*

* In his memoir, "I Remember, I Remember", M. Maurois relates how quite unintentionally he fathered a new type of biography which in recent years has been quite popular, but at the same time has been the subject of

*Agony and the Ecstasy* by Irving Stone. Here we have biographical fact embroidered and embellished by the imagination and gift of story-telling of the novelist. Such books, says Dr. Collins, are "easy reading, mildly instructive, and moderately diverting . . . a good substitute for fiction and a fairly acceptable one for history."

*Panegyric*—this is not so much a class of biographies as a quality of some biographical writing. The term means eulogistic and applies, of course, to those works which are wholly laudatory and uncritical.

And now for the questions which a reviewer may ask of a biography—questions the answers to which will form the substance of his review—

*Does the book give a full-length picture of the subject?*

Some books may deal only with a period in a man's life, or a phase of his career. David Ogilvy's *Confessions of an Advertising Man,* for example, is devoted wholly to his work in this field and has little of a personal nature in it.

*What phases of the subject's life receive greatest space? Is there justification for this?*

---

some criticism. He was advised, he reports, to explain in the preface of *Ariel,* his life of Shelley, just what he had tried to accomplish in this book. "No doubt this was a mistake," he writes, "for from this brief preface was born, much against my intention, the absurd and dangerous expression: 'romanticized biography'. I had never used it; I had on the contrary said that a biographer has no right to invent either a fact or a speech, but that he should arrange his authentic materials in the manner of a novel and give his reader the feeling of a hero's progressive discovery of the world which is the essence of romance. But few people take the trouble to read carefully, especially prefaces, and the success of *Ariel,* a success which astonished my publisher and me, encouraged a whole series of 'Romantic Lives' and 'Private Lives' which were often very bad. For some time I suffered from the reaction against this avalanche of improvised biographies and I took great care, when I myself returned to this type of book, to respect the legitimate phobias of meticulous, distrustful, and atrabiliar men of learning . . . ."

*What is the point of view of the author?*

The answers to these questions may well be illustrated by some of the innumerable biographies of Woodrow Wilson. One of these is by David Lawrence, who was a student of Wilson's at Princeton, who reported his activities as governor of New Jersey, who covered the White House, and who accompanied him on his peace missions to Europe. Another is by Joseph P. Tumulty, for years Wilson's personal secretary. Yet others are by Josephus Daniels a member of Wilson's cabinet, Arthur S. Link, Professor of History at Princeton, and Thomas A. Bailey, Professor of History at Stanford. Each of these had an approach to Wilson, an understanding and explanation of the man, and a point of view and an emphasis in his biography which were different from all the others. And in each case, it is as much the authorship as what is said about the subject that gives the book charm and distinction. This is often the case in biographies of a person who is much written about. (We might also consider some of the recent books on President John F. Kennedy here—notably, *Kennedy* by Theodore C. Sorensen, a close friend and Special Counsel to Kennedy; *A Thousand Days* by Arthur Schlesinger, Jr., Special Assistant to Kennedy; *John F. Kennedy, President* by Hugh Sidey, described as "the reporter closest to Kennedy"; *My Twelve Years with John F. Kennedy* by Evelyn Lincoln, his personal secretary, etc.)

*Are peculiarities, idiosyncrasies, weaknesses, foibles, and the like omitted, treated adequately, or over-played?*

In the campaign biography, personality deficiencies will undoubtedly be omitted. In fictionized and debunking biography, they are sometimes over-played, especially if they be such as to contribute to what has been called "time-denatured scandal." The middle ground—neither omission nor exaggeration—is, of course, the ideal which conscientious biographers seek.

*How is the subject-matter organized?*

Ordinarily, biographies follow one or two orders—chronological or news style. In the latter case, the book opens with something dramatic rather than with the traditional hereditary background of the subject. Just as the most important information in a news story is placed in the first paragraph (called the *lead,* in newspaper parlance), so in some biographies the opening chapter features those aspects of a subject's life that give the book a *raison d'être.* In "The Elephant's Child," Rudyard Kipling wrote a poem in which these lines appear:

> *"I keep six honest serving-men;*
> *(They taught me all I knew)*
> *Their names are What and Why and When*
> *And How and Where and Who."*

In some biographies, the answers to *Who? Why? Where? When? What?* and *How?* are played up in the opening chapters. The hereditary background in such cases is sandwiched into subsequent parts of the narrative. This arrangement often makes for greater readability, and is not necessarily confusing chronologically.

*Is the treatment superficial, or does the author show extensive study into the subject's life?*

A campaign biography is often superficial, whereas a biography done as a thesis or dissertation for a higher academic degree is likely to be a work of scholarship.

*What source materials were used in the preparation of this book?*

*Is the work documented?*

In all biographical and historical writing, original source material is valued above secondary sources. The reviewer can ordinarily determine the kind of source material used by a biographer from his introduction, appendix, footnotes, or the text itself. If a biographer has access to rare documents of any sort, he will undoubtedly make reference to these, and they may well be worth mentioning in the review. There is a tendency away from documentation in biographies intended for popular consumption. Publishers feel that books with footnotes are not attractive to the ordinary lay reader. In such cases, the documentation is either in an appendix or skillfully worked into the text itself.

*Does the author endeavor to get at hidden motives?*

This question should recall the comment about Gamaliel Bradford and *psychography*. All but the more superficial biographers are concerned to some extent with the motivations of personality—what makes an individual "tick."

Critic and biographer Leon Edel, whose biography of Henry James was awarded a Pulitzer Prize and a National Book Award, points out:*

"The biographer may be as imaginative as he pleases—the more imaginative the better—in the way in which he brings his materials together. But he must not imagine the materials. He must read himself into the past; but then he must read that past into our present. He must read himself into the life he is writing; but he must beware of re-creating that life in his own image. He must judge the facts but not

* "That One May Say This Was the Man", *Opinions and Perspectives from the New York Times Book Review,* edited by Francis Brown, Houghton Mifflin.

sit in judgment. He must respect the dead—but he must tell the truth."

*What important new facts about the subject's life are revealed in the book?*

All biographers, especially those of individuals who have been the subjects of several studies, are supposed to reveal something new, either in fact or in interpretation. The *news* of a biography may well be the feature of the review, particularly if it be intended for newspaper publication. (Many reviewers of Elizabeth Longford's *Queen Victoria: Born to Succeed* pointed out that Lady Longford had been given access—for the first time—to all relevant papers in the Royal Archives.)

*What is the relationship of the subject's career to contemporary history?*

Biographer John A. Garraty remarks:* "Every biographer, as he settles down at his desk, must make certain basic decisions before he begins to write. Shall he do a long 'definitive' study or a brief survey? Shall he simply delineate his subject's actions, or strike out boldly and try to explain the significance of these actions? Shall he emphasize his hero's career, or stress his personality and the intimacies of his private life? In part, the biographer's decisions will depend on his philosophy of history. If, for instance, he feels that the times make the man, he will emphasize the environment and tend to show how it influenced his hero's seemingly independent judgments and decisions."

No individual exists in a vacuum, much less one who is

* "How Should You Tell a Man's Story", *Opinions and Perspectives from the New York Times Book Review,* edited by Francis Brown, Houghton Mifflin.

sufficiently important to be the subject of a biography. As Shakespeare wrote, "All the world's a stage, and all the men and women merely players." The subject of a biography has undoubtedly, to some extent, shaped or has been influenced by the passing scene, and the reviewer, just as the biographer, should comment on this.

Reference should be made to the historical reliability of the book and its contribution to a better understanding of the period of the subject's life.

*Is the subject of the biography still living?*

The answer to this question has a bearing not only on the review, but on the biography itself.

*How does this biography compare with others about the same person?*

*How does it compare with other works by the same author?*

Comparison is, of course, a useful device in exposition. The reviewer should not, however, make invidious comparisons.

The review of a biography should be as interesting as the book itself—possibly more so, because the review will be shorter and the writer should have quite a wealth of material from which he may select points to be treated in his article. Many reviews of biographies are in themselves excellent sketches of the subjects of the biographies. All might well be such.

In conclusion, the reviewer may well keep in mind that biography today, in the opinion of M. Maurois, is distinctive in at least three ways:

1. It is more courageous and more uncompromising in its search for facts about a subject and for a completely honest interpretation of them.

2. Modern biography tends to emphasize, as Dostoievsky did in the novel, the "multiplicity of vital energy at the heart of a single soul."

3. It lays emphasis on the struggle that necessarily goes on within the complex nature.

"The modern biographer," says M. Maurois, "if he is honest, will not allow himself to think: 'Here is a great king, a great statesman, a great writer; round his name a legend has been built; it is on the legend, and the legend alone, that I wish to dwell.' No. He thinks rather: 'Here is a man. I possess a certain number of documents, a certain amount of evidence about him. I am going to draw a true portrait. What will this portrait be? I have no idea. I don't want to know before I have actually drawn it. I am prepared to accept whatever a prolonged contemplation of my subject may reveal to me, and to correct it in proportion to such new facts as I discover.' "

Dr. Collins stated the case for biography well when he wrote that "next to poetry, biography is the most satisfying reading of all ages: instructive to youth, inspiring to maturity, solacing to old age. Its human interest, its preoccupation with man, brings it close to our understanding and to our emotions."

# VI
# HISTORY

*I have read somewhere or other,—in Dionysius of Halicarnassus, I think,—that history is philosophy teaching by examples.*

—Viscount Bolingbroke.

*History is the essence of innumerable biographies.*

*Nothing that was worthy in the past departs; no truth or goodness realized by man ever dies, or can die; but is all still here, and, recognized or not, lives and works through endless changes.*

—Thomas Carlyle.

## HISTORY

HISTORY AND BIOGRAPHY are very much alike. It is simply a matter of emphasis. Thomas Heywood once wrote:

> *"The world's a theatre, the earth a stage,*
> *Which God and Nature do with actors fill."*

In the case of biography, the spotlight is on the actor. In history, the entire stage is illuminated. The individual is still important, but only as he and his acts fit into the larger pattern of the stage and drama as a whole.

Which means that many of the questions and suggestions for the reviewing of biography are also applicable to history. There are, however, additional guideposts.

Dr. Allan Nevins, the Pulitzer-prize-winning writer, editor, scholar, and teacher, has observed that authors who deal with history may be divided as was all Gaul—into three parts. There are the pedants who dominate the historical landscape, and who never have nor ever will write with understanding and with feeling. There are the popularizers who sacrifice everything meaningful . . . for the sake of getting their stuff published. And there are those few who try, successfully or otherwise, to combine literary skill with scholarly production.

The authorship of works of history is, therefore, the first point the reviewer should note.

Not only who is the author, but *what training has he had for this kind of work?*

It is interesting to note that some of our most widely read and highly praised histories have been written, not by the professors of history, but by journalists. John Gunther, who wrote *Roosevelt in Retrospect, The Riddle of MacArthur* and the famous "Inside" books, was a reporter and foreign correspondent; Richard H. Rovere is a staff writer for *The New Yorker* as well as the author of *Affairs of State: The Eisenhower Years,* etc.; foreign correspondent and editor Theodore H. White has written two *Making of the President* books plus others in various fields; Barbara W. Tuchman, author of *The Guns of August,* etc., was a magazine staff writer and foreign correspondent.

The foregoing comment is not meant to imply that the professional historians have not produced some excellent popular treatises, because they have. Samuel Eliot Morison with his *Oxford History of the American People* and Bruce Catton with his *The Coming Fury, Terrible Swift Sword* and *Never Call Retreat* (volumes of *The Centennial History of the Civil War*) are excellent examples.

Other questions for reviewers of works of history to note are—

*What else has the author of this volume written?*

*How did the public and the critics react to his previous work?*

Some writers of history build up an enthusiastic following. Readers await the new books eagerly. For instance, Will and Ariel Durant have done a highly popular series; the ninth volume of Dr. and Mrs. Durant's *Story of Civilization* was titled *The Age of Voltaire* and was a Book-of-the-Month Club selection recently.

*With what particular period does the book deal?*

The very nature of historical research necessitates limitations in time and space. The tendency in assignments for graduate theses and dissertations, out of which many books of history grow, is in this direction.

*How thorough is the treatment?*

*What seem to have been the sources used?*

Sources and documentation are as important in histories as in biographies. Barbara W. Tuchman, writing in *Harper's Magazine,* notes: "Ideas alone are not flesh and blood. Too often, scholarly history is written in terms of ideas rather than acts; it tells what people wrote instead of what they performed. To write, say, a history of progressivism in America or of socialism in the era of the Second International by quoting the editorials, books, articles, speeches and so forth of the leading figures is easy. They were the wordiest people in history. If, however, one checks what they said and wrote against what actually was happening, a rather different picture emerges. . . . People out of power always talk more than those who have power. The historian must be careful to guard against this phenomenon—weight it, as the statisticians say—lest his result be unbalanced."

*Is the account given in broad outline, or in detail?*

A comparison of James Truslow Adams' *The Epic of America* and David Saville Muzzey's *The American Adventure* will illustrate the point. One is a single volume. The other consists of two large volumes, in smaller type. Both tell essentially the same story, but one contains much greater detail than the other.

*Is the style essentially that of reportorial writing, or is there an effort at interpretative writing?*

Textbooks tend to be more objective than the histories

which are intended for general reading or for consumption by other historians.

*What seems to be the point of view or thesis of the author?*

Truth, of course, should be the goal in all historical writing, just as in other fields of research. Manipulation of facts to establish a point is nothing short of distortion. Nonetheless, there is such a thing as an honest thesis or point of view in historical interpretation. Charles A. Beard with his economic interpretation is probably the best known example. Dr. Beard's attitude—an inquiry into real motives and the cold facts of historical action—has certainly made itself felt in historiography and has contributed to a more truthful interpretation of America's past. Mrs. Tuchman comments, "It is more rewarding . . . to assemble the facts first and, in the process of arranging them in narrative form, to discover a theory or a historical generalization emerging of its own accord. This to me is the excitement, the built-in treasure hunt, of writing history."

*Is the treatment superficial or profound?*

The superficial is easier to detect than the spuriously profound. Dr. Nevins has observed that many historians go down into the well of scholarship and never come up, yet all the while they send up messages of complaint about the worthlessness of the work of others. The reviewer should look with suspicion on anything that appears too glib or too profound.

*For what group is the book intended?*

Publishers, in thinking of the markets for history books, usually have in mind these groups: (a) textbooks for schools and colleges, (b) popular treatises for the general trade, and (c) scholarly treatises for libraries and students of history —lay and professional.

*What part does biographical writing play in the book?*

Previous comments on the relationship of biography and history are applicable here.

*Does the book emphasize the traditional subject-matter of history—wars, kings, politicians, etc., or is it social history?*

Editor and historian Eric Larrabee noted in a review in *Harper's Magazine*, "The history of any people, until very recently, was in the main anonymous. Formal history has fortunately begun to recognize the need to dig it out, to reconstruct however imperfectly some notion of how life was lived by those unfortunate (or fortunate) enough to inhabit the background of great events. Their tools and their buildings, their dreams and their daily trivia, will increasingly become legitimate raw material for the historian, not simply as ornaments to an otherwise bald, politico-economic narrative, but as proper subjects for study and reflection."

Dr. Nevins has reported:*

"This much at least is clear: the wealth of content available is matched by an enrichment of the implements for penetrating and explaining it. All the social studies—anthropology, psychology, economics, sociology, political science, social geography (to use a better term than human geography)—have been made handmaidens of history. When one of the groups that cooperated to establish the magazine *American Heritage,* itself one of the remarkable achievements of our time in the historical field, made tests of public taste, it laid before a large body of potential readers a choice among three emphases. Would they prefer narrative and descriptive articles interesting simply for color, drama and

* "The Telling of a Nation's Story", *Opinions and Perspectives from the New York Times Book Review,* edited by Francis Brown, Houghton Mifflin.

suspense? Or articles presenting history with an implied application to present-day events, like 'The Arab World in Early American Diplomacy'? Or articles that dealt with important forces and events as reinterpreted by use of various social studies?—say 'Battle Fatigue in the Civil War' as viewed by an expert psychologist. The largest vote was for the third category. Even average readers wanted the latest ideas of experts applied to the past."

*Are dates used extensively, and if so, are they used intelligently?*

The story is told—it may be apocryphal—that one of Harvard's great historians, none other than the eminent Henry Adams, could never remember such elementary dates as 1492 or 1776. It has also been pointed out that many of our most widely read and most worthwhile histories—books such as *The Epic of America*—have few dates, and these are not given great emphasis. All of which is just another way of saying that dates—school memories to the contrary notwithstanding—are not all of history, and should be no more than guideposts to keep one moving properly along the highway of time.

*Is the book likely soon to be out of date, or is it written so as to stand the test of time?*

Books often are hastily written and rushed through the press so as to tie in with some subject in the news. While such works may undoubtedly serve a worthwhile current purpose, their usefulness is likely to be short-lived.

*Is this book a revision and if so, how does it compare with previous editions?*

Appearance of a new edition usually means one of two things: (1) There is a greater demand for the book than the first printing would satisfy, or (2) the author has added new material or made other changes in the content.

*Are maps, illustrations, charts, etc., used and how may these be evaluated?*

In some books—the Horizon Caravel books issued by American Heritage Publishing Company, for example—the illustrative material is almost as interesting and valuable as the text. With the ever-increasing emphasis on pictorial journalism and education (see such magazines as *Life* and *Look* and the tenets of progressive education), reviewers may well pay some attention to this subject in their comments on history.

# VII

# CONTEMPORARY THOUGHT

*Reading is concentrated living. It is a shortcut to the abundant life. It is everyman's experience made your own. Reading explains, improves, and intensifies living.*

—Charles Lee.

*All that mankind has done, thought, gained, or been—it is lying as in magic preservation in the pages of books.*

—Thomas Carlyle.

# CONTEMPORARY THOUGHT

BOOKS ON CONTEMPORARY THOUGHT include current treatises on economics, government, religion, philosophy, sociology, the sciences, and similar subjects.

Books in this category are similar to speeches, essays, or other subjective utterances, and can best be reviewed, therefore, in the same manner that addresses are covered in the news columns of the public press.

Which is just another way of saying that the technique of the speech report is the technique of the review of a book on contemporary thought.

There are two major problems in the speech report:

(1) Getting exact words for use as direct quotations, and,

(2) Condensing long utterances without losing proportion, balance, etc.

In the solution of both problems, there are certain dangers against which the reviewer should be on guard:*

1. Unintentional distortion which may come about by giving disproportionate space to certain points.

2. The playing up of statements, which apart from their context are misleading.

3. Inaccuracy or untruthfulness (there is a difference between accuracy and truthfulness) as a result of carelessness in copying material for quotation purposes.

* An adaptation from *Newspaper Writing and Editing,* by W. G. Bleyer, Houghton Mifflin Co.

4. Misrepresentation which derives from bias, prejudice, political or philosophical partisanship.

The solution of the first problem of the speech report, viz., getting exact words, offers no difficulty in the review of a book on contemporary thought. It is simply a matter of marking passages as one reads and copying these accurately as the review is written.

As for the second problem—condensing long utterances, it should be remembered that the review, despite its comparative brevity, should give an adequate picture both of the book and the subject of the volume.

Just as the lead (opening paragraph or paragraphs) of a news story is a summary of the entire article, so should the review of a book on contemporary thought provide the essence or gist of the author's discourse.

The review should not be limited to one or more striking points, but rather should cover all the major concepts—more succinctly, and without the detail of the book, of course.

The reviewer will be aided in determining the main points in a book on contemporary thought by studying the author's purpose and plan, by reading his introduction carefully, by noting the pattern of his narrative as revealed in the table of contents, and by detecting summarizing statements in concluding portions of chapters and at the end of the book itself.

The introduction of a review in this field may be:

1. A direct quotation of a single sentence.
2. A direct quotation of a paragraph.
3. An indirect quotation of a sentence.
4. An indirect quotation of a paragraph.
5. The keynote or gist of the book.
6. The title, particularly if quite descriptive or otherwise

distinctive. (For example, *The American Way of Death* by Jessica Mitford.)

7. The name of the author.

8. Conditions surrounding the inception, publication, or release of the book.

9. Some association with an item or items in the news.

Any one of these may also be the theme of the entire review.

The body of the review will consist of carefully chosen, directly quoted sentences and paragraphs, held together by summarizing paragraphs.

Or stated another way, the body of the review will be a series of summarizing units, vivified, illustrated, accentuated, and given life, color, and action by carefully chosen passages which are quoted directly.

In all paragraphs where direct quotations are used, such expressions as "the author said," "Mr. ——— explained," "the book brings out," etc., should be included.

Such explanatory clauses should be used in paragraphs of summary or indirect quotation when the clarity of the unit so demands.

These expressions should be sandwiched into paragraphs so as not to be conspicuous in themselves. They should not come at the beginning of paragraphs, but rather at the end or the middle.

Some appropriate synonyms for the word *say* for use in this connection are: explain, insist, ask, advocate, demand, point out, discuss, consider, expostulate, discourse, elucidate, describe, assert, and claim.

As for questions that may be asked and answered in a review of a book of contemporary thought, here are some:

*Is the subject-matter or the style more important?*

Outstanding among books on contemporary thought are the *Prejudices* series by H. L. Mencken. In these—some six volumes—the vitriolic former editor of *The American Mercury* comments caustically on a wide variety of themes. Much of what he says is sound. Some of it is in the nature of half-truths. All of it is highly entertaining because of the way in which it is phrased. In the language which A. G. Gardiner, eminent British editor, used to characterize Dean Inge:

"His insults have a flavor that makes you lap them up with gusto, and before you have time to be angry with him for his savage assaults on your pet enthusiasms, you have forgiven him for some smashing blow that he has struck at your pet aversion."

Which means that in the case of Mencken's writings, just as in many other works on contemporary thought, style is as worthy of the reviewer's notice as the content.

*Who is the author, and what right has he to be writing on this subject?*

Authorship, as has been pointed out in other sections, is important in any type of book. For books on contemporary thought, which are largely subjective or based on study and research in a particular field, the qualifications of the author have added significance. A book on the current political scene by Richard Rovere commands respect because Mr. Rovere is a noted political commentator and a staff writer with *The New Yorker* who has contributed the "Letter from Washington" to that magazine since 1948. Such a book as *The Secret of Victorious Living* or *Twelve Tests of Character* is given careful consideration because it has been written by the distinguished religious scholar and minister of the Riverside Church, New York, Dr. Harry Emerson Fosdick.

In similar fashion, books on literature by Edmund Wilson or on philosophy by Harry and Bonaro Overstreet rely on authorship for one of their claims to distinction.

*What seems to have been the author's purpose in writing this book?*

Many books in this field are simply to inform—to pass on to the largest possible reading public new facts or new points of view. Others are intended to interpret, to explain, to give new meaning to old themes, possibly in the light of recent discoveries of scholarship or the laboratory. Yet other books on contemporary thought are motivated by something akin to the zeal of the evangelist. Their authors have a message to impart, and the printed page is their medium.

An author's preface, the pattern of the book itself, and comment in technical and scientific journals are all possible keys to purpose.

*What contributions to knowledge and understanding are made by this book?*

Such a question as this implies a knowledge on the part of the reviewer of the field represented by the volume. As a quick means of reviewing the essential facts on a given subject, the encyclopedia and other reference books can be put to good use in this connection. An author's preface will sometimes point to new material or new interpretations in the volume.

Especially in the case of scientific books, the reviewer should be on his guard not to let anything spurious pass undetected. Many of the better newspapers and magazines will not entrust a scientific book for review to anyone who does not have a rather good scientific background, acquired through academic training. When one feels that his knowledge of a field represented by a new book is too limited to make possible a sound evaluation of the volume, he can simply fall back on the principles of straight reporting. He will, in this case, merely relate what the author is writing, and will offer no criticism, directly or indirectly.

The structure of a review of a book on contemporary thought seldom follows the order of the chapters in the book. The review will feature in the lead or introduction the items of greatest interest or importance. These may be scattered throughout the book or may be summarized in a concluding chapter. The pattern of the review will likely be that of the news story, viz., the inverted pyramid, with the contents moving from the most important to the least important item.

A review in this field must satisfy two groups: (1) the lay public, which will read the review only if it be an interesting, informative article in itself, and (2) the specialist, who will insist on accuracy, truthfulness, and an intelligent appraisal of the relative merits of this book as compared to others in the field.

# VIII

# TRAVEL AND ADVENTURE

*The pleasure of travel, which only exists as a matter of fact in retrospect and seldom in the present, at the instant when it is being experienced.*

*One could revel, for instance, in long explorations while near one's own fireside, stimulating the restive or the sluggish mind, if need be, by reading some narrative of travel in distant lands.*

—Joris Karl Huysmans.

*All our adventures were by the fireside, and all our migrations from the blue bed to the brown.*

—Oliver Goldsmith.

## TRAVEL AND ADVENTURE

HOW MAY we account for the popularity of books of travel and adventure?

Or, stated another way, who are the many readers of this type of literature?

There are at least three large groups:

1. Almost everyone is interested to some extent in travel books. There are not many of us who at one time or another have not wanted to travel to faraway places. Since few of us can follow this desire, we turn to books for vicarious adventure.

2. There are those who read travel and adventure books for definite information on the peoples of various parts of the world—students of particular races, countries, customs, etc. At the time of this writing, for example, there is much interest in Africa, and many books are being issued about the continent—*Africa: A Natural History* by Leslie Brown, *Politics in West Africa* by W. Arthur Lewis, and *The Savage State* by Georges Conchon (recent winner of France's *Prix Goncourt*).

3. Yet another group interested in books of travel and adventure are the hobbyists who collect books and maps about their favorite sections of the globe. These range from the amateur to the discerning bibliophile.

To open a travel book with high expectation, only to find it dull, is probably worse than not to read at all. Which means that a major function of the reviewer is to present in full flavor the best travel books and to warn his readers of the flat or sensationally untrue books.

Questions which will aid the reviewer in appraising books in this category are:

*Just what is meant by a book of travel and adventure?*

Books in this category cover a wide range. One readily identifies such volumes as *Spring on an Arctic Island* by Katharine Scherman, *Americans on Everest* by James Ramsey Ullman, or *London on Sunday* by Betty James as belonging to this classification. But what about such a volume as John Steinbeck's *Travels with Charley* or *Westviking* by Farley Mowat? Or the many books by foreign correspondents, including *The Italians: Face of a Nation* by John Phillips and Vincent Sheean's *Personal History*? Actually, all of these, different as they are, are books of travel and adventure. Some—and this is often the case with books in this field—may also be classified as biography or contemporary thought. Questions and suggestions for reviews in these categories are, therefore, partially applicable to travel and adventure.

*What about the credibility of the writer?*

Authorship is important in any kind of book, but in a class where there are many opportunities for grandiose tales and few means of checking on the truthfulness of such yarns, it is doubly important that the author's reliability be established. Biographical facts and references to other books by him will aid the reviewer in this connection.

*What is the purpose of the book?*

*What is the author's pattern for the accomplishment of this purpose?*

Books on travel or adventure range from the thriller, intended merely for entertainment, to the technical contribution to geography and other sciences. So far as the lay public is concerned, the ideal is probably best described as being for the book world what the *National Geographic Magazine* is for the periodical world, viz., a medium for the popularizing of geographic and scientific knowledge. Writers in this field should not find it necessary to sacrifice scientific accuracy or to resort to the ephemeral, exotic, or sensational.

*What does the book contain that is new both in content and in treatment?*

This question implies the value of background to the reviewer in this field, just as in others. It also suggests that many travel and adventure books deal with themes that have previously been handled by other authors, and that the best review will be produced by the person who familiarizes himself with these works.

*What specific contributions does this volume make to man's knowledge of geography, government, economics, folklore, customs, etc.?*

Here again background will be helpful. So will a careful reading of the preface. Authors, proud of their brain-children, will often comment on a volume's particular contributions to human knowledge and its other claims to distinction. A reading of the section on the subject of the book in some good encyclopedia, such as the *Britannica,* prior to examination of the book, is yet another way to arrive at the answer to this question.

*Does the book have news value?*

Were a person very much in the public eye to make an adventurous journey and, upon his return, were he to write a book about it, the book would undoubtedly be news.

Richard Halliburton and his many excellent travel and adventure books would be a good example. This author was often in the news. Such books as *The Royal Road to Romance, The Glorious Adventure, New Worlds to Conquer, The Flying Carpet,* and *Seven League Boots* enjoyed what the French call "a good press," and sold extremely well, largely because coincidental with their appearance the author was making front-page headlines by swimming the Hellespont, or retracing the routes of Alexander, Balboa, Cortes, Hannibal, and Ulysses. Mr. Halliburton's death, in fact, was in keeping with the theme of his books. While en route from China to San Francisco, the Chinese junk in which he was traveling disappeared. The news stories at the time stimulated renewed interest in all his books.

If the book be a translation, something of the translator and his methods should be told in the review. Comparisons with other books on the same subject and by the same author will also help. Within its limits, a review in this field should be a travel article, interesting in itself, and entirely capable of standing on its own feet.

# IX

# FICTION

*"And what are you reading, Miss——?" "Oh! it is only a novel!" replies the young lady: while she lays down her book with affected indifference, or momentary shame.—"It is only Cecilia, or Camilla, or Belinda:" or, in short, only some work in which the most thorough knowledge of human nature, the happiest delineation of its varieties, the liveliest effusions of wit and humour are conveyed to the world in the best chosen language.*

—Jane Austen.

*The only obligation to which in advance we may hold a novel, without incurring the obligation of being arbitrary, is that it be interesting.*

—Henry James.

## FICTION

IF THERE BE any dominant injunction for the reviewer of fiction, it is this:

*Do not give away the story.*

In the language of Edward Weeks, editor of *The Atlantic Monthly*, "The woman who sits behind you at the theatre and who, thanks to a previous visit, thinks she must warn you of everything that is going to happen is no more of a bore than the reviewer who devotes half his space to telling you a skeletonized version of the plot. In each case your informant is removing every vestige of surprise from a performance, much of whose entertainment is derived from the fact that the audience doesn't know what's coming next. I have inveighed against a certain superiority in reviewers: I really think that the man who gives the story away is quite as much of a nuisance. Even the ablest critics are sometimes guilty of this fallacy. Booksellers and publishers both know that people read primarily to be amused, and it makes them furious to see the contents of a promising new novel (which has taken the author ten months and 360 pages to build up) predigested in three dry paragraphs by an uninspired reviewer. The only people who profit from such stupid reviewing are those who like to talk about books they haven't read."

The reviewer of fiction will be aided in his work if he will bear in mind the reasons which lead to the reading of novels. There are a number of these, some of which are:

1. Many persons seek in the vicarious realm of fiction wider and more unusual experiences than their positions in society will permit. They go places and do things as they read a book which would otherwise be impossible. Such individuals often imagine themselves the hero or heroine, or some other character in the book, and get quite a thrill therefrom.

2. Some persons read fiction for escape. To them it is a literary narcotic, and, in its way, may be as habit-forming and as harmful as alcohol or morphine. This is especially true of young people and others who have a tendency to withdraw from society into themselves. Some types of fiction are more harmful in this connection than others.

Bliss Perry writes on this subject:*

"Fiction . . . chosen for its power to afford distraction or even dissipation to an overwrought mind, unquestionably serves a useful purpose, though it need scarcely be said that an exclusive reliance upon trivial and sensational stories as furnishing mental relaxation is an indication of poverty of intellectual resources."

3. There are yet other persons who read fiction so as to be able to talk interestingly about the new novels and their authors. Many of these individuals are genuinely interested in good literature, while others go about their reading in much the spirit that they would eat spinach or take out an accident or life insurance policy.

4. Some persons like to read fiction which deals with subjects in which they are especially interested. Teachers, for example, may enjoy novels that take place in schools, such as *The Rector of Justin* by Louis Auchincloss or *Up the Down Staircase* by Bel Kaufman. *The Source* by James A.

* From *A Study of Prose Fiction*, by Bliss Perry, Houghton Mifflin Co.

Michener and *The Mandelbaum Gate* by Muriel Spark would appeal to readers interested in reading about Israel. And those who enjoy politics might want to read such novels as Irving Wallace's *The Man,* Allen Drury's *Advise and Consent* or *Seven Days in May* by Fletcher Knebel and Charles W. Bailey.

5. There is that small but discriminating group, always appreciative of the good and the beautiful, who turn to the better novels in the spirit of the connoisseur—one who, in the words of the dictionary definition, is competent to act as a critical judge of an art, or in a matter of taste. These are the ones who, in the language of Guy de Maupassant, say to the novelist: "Make for me something *fine,* in the form which suits you best, following your own temperament."

6. And, finally, there is that large group—the bulk of the fiction readers—who are seeking nothing more than entertainment. These are the ones who go to the movies by the millions, who flock to Atlantic City and Miami in season, and who watch television with fidelity. They are the ones who, to quote de Maupassant again, ask of the novelist: "Console me, amuse me,—make me sad,—make me sentimental,—make me dream,—make me laugh,—make me tremble,—make me weep,—make me think."

Although the terms *novel* and *novelist* are generally used synonymously with the word *fiction,* actually the *novel* is but one of several fictional forms. Other widely recognized forms include the *short story,* the *novelette,* and the *novella.*

The *novel* is defined in Webster's as "an invented prose narrative of considerable length and a certain complexity that deals imaginatively with human experience through a connected sequence of events involving a group of persons in a specific setting."

The *novelette* is defined by William Rose Benét in *The Reader's Encyclopedia* (Crowell) as "a long short story." Mr. Benét adds, "Of 15,000 words or somewhat more, it is less considerable in length than the novella."

The *novella* is currently a popular form. (The 1960 National Book Award for fiction was awarded to Philip Roth for his collection, *Goodbye, Columbus,* which contained a novella—from which the book takes its title—and five short stories.) Mr. Benét comments that the term novella "is used in English to designate a serious fictional form that is somewhere between the novel and the short story in length. Also sometimes called the nouvelle, the novella probably contains from 30,000 to 40,000 words, as compared to a full novel of a minimum of 60,000 words, and often of twice that and more."

The *short story* is defined by Karl Beckson and Arthur Ganz (in *A Reader's Guide to Literary Terms*: Farrar, Straus) as "a prose narrative briefer than a short novel, more restricted in characters and situations, and usually concerned with a single effect. Unlike longer forms of fiction, the short story does not develop character fully; generally, a single aspect of personality undergoes change or is revealed as the result of conflict. . . . Because of limited length, the background against which the characters move is generally sketched lightly."

As a reviewer of fiction goes about his task, he can with profit recall that there are four essential elements to the novel, each of which should be appraised with care:

1. The characters,
2. The plot (or theme),
3. The setting or background, and
4. The style.

With reference to the first, a reviewer may well ask—

*What are the sources of the novelist's characters?*

Characters may be based on persons known to or observed by the novelist, although usually, as set forth at the first of novels and movies, their identities are veiled so as not to make them readily known to the book or theatre public.

Characters may also be based on something the author has read or on historical figures. In the historical novel or in fictionized biography, such personae are to be found.

Characters, yet again, may be figments of the imagination of the novelist. This is especially true in the more bizarre or fantastic type of story.

Not only may the reviewer ask about the sources of character, but he should also determine the attitude of the writer toward his characters.

*Does the novelist apparently look with pride upon the beauty, strength, or other virtues of his creations?*

*On the other hand, is his attitude one of contempt or hostility?*

*Or, does he take a compromise position, limiting himself to a sympathetic delineation of his brain children?*

All of which suggests other questions about the author's technique in character delineation.

*Is the direct or the indirect plan used?*

In the first, an author, to quote Bliss Perry, "narrates their actions, reports their words, or by one of the immemorial conventions of the story-teller's craft, he tells us what is lurking in their thoughts."

In the indirect delineation, a hero, for example, is not depicted as such, but rather the reader is shown how his acts so affect others that they think of him in terms of heroism. As Mr. Perry has written, "the more subtle, the more psychological the particular work of fiction happens to be, the greater become the possibilities of the indirect method of character delineation."

With further reference to characters, the reviewer will observe that some characters are simple and others complex. Some characters are stationary and others develop. Character development is based largely, of course, on struggle. Victory, not defeat, is the goal, but the goal is not always achieved. "Some of the most famous examples of character-drawing in modern fiction represent . . . not moral victory but defeat," writes Mr. Perry. "To watch a character deteriorate, no matter how strongly he battles against adversity of circumstances or inherent weakness of nature, imparts to fiction the tragedy of actual life."

The term *plot* means the plan or main story of a literary composition comprising a complication, or causally connected series of motivated incidents, which are gradually unfolded, sometimes by unexpected means.

Plot also grows out of an author's own observation, his memory of something he has read or heard, or his own inventiveness. Questions relative to plot which a reviewer may well ask would include such as the following:*

*How are the various elements of plot, such as introduction, suspense, climax, and conclusion, handled in this story?*

*What is the relationship of plot to character delineation?*

*What devices of plot are employed to aid in character delineation?*

*Is catastrophe introduced for plot purposes?*

*To what extent, and how, is accident employed as a complicating and/or resolving force?*

* An adaptation of suggestions for study by Bliss Perry in *A Study of Prose Fiction,* Houghton Mifflin.

*Is fate used?*

*What about mystery?*

*What other devices of plot complication and resolution are employed?*

*Is there a sub-plot, and how is this related to the main plot?*

*Is there more than one sub-plot?*

*Is plot primary or secondary to some of the other essential elements of the story, viz., characters, setting, or style?*

Setting or background has the same origins as character and plot, viz., the author's observation, reading, or imagination.

The term may apply to atmosphere, locale, or scenic effects.

Setting may be historical, or local color (regional or sectional), occupational or institutional, or, as in the case of highly subjective psychological novels, ethereal and esoteric.

The fiction reader should, of course, pay close attention to setting or background and should comment on this in his review. He should note its relationship to character delineation and to the action of the plot.

As for style, the reviewer may well distinguish between the elements and qualities of language.

Elements of style include words, figures of speech, sentences, and paragraphs.

Qualities include (a) the intellectual qualities of simplicity and clearness; (b) the emotional qualities of pathos, humor, force, tragedy, pity, etc.; and (c) the aesthetic qualities of melody, harmony, taste, rhythm, and beauty.

In a consideration of style, the reviewer may also note how the novelist employs the standard rhetorical devices of narration, description, exposition, and argumentation.

J. Scott Clark in his *A Study of English Prose Writers: A Laboratory Method* (Scribner's) employs a plan which may be adapted by reviewers. In his section on Dickens' style, for example, he has a list of peculiar characteristics as pointed out by competent critics, each characteristic being illustrated by extracts from the novels. These are grouped thus:

"1. Fondness for Caricature—Exaggeration—Grotesqueness. 2. Genial Humor. 3. Incarnation of Characteristics—Single Strokes. 4. Descriptive Power—Minuteness of Observation—Vividness. 5. Tender, sometimes Mawkish, Pathos. 6. Gayety—Animal Spirits—Good-Fellowship. 7. Sincerity—Manliness—Earnestness. 8. Broad Sympathy—Plain, Practical Humanity. 9. Dramatic Power. 10. Vulgarity—Artificiality. 11. Diffuseness."

The novel may be approached, of course, on the basis of content and/or as an art form. It may also be considered in such terms as purpose, type, and realism. The last is a term often heard. To many persons, it is synonymous with the sordid, the unpleasant, the disreputable. Realism to some means *Tobacco Road* or worse. Actually there is the realism of the sunrise or the sunset just as there is the realism of the pigsty or the abattoir. Realism can be pleasant as well as unpleasant.

In a chapter on the reviewing of fiction, there should, perhaps, be a brief word about the detective story—a literary form the importance of which is indicated by both the number and the diversity of its readers.

Howard Haycraft, in his *Murder for Pleasure: The Life and Times of the Detective Story* (Appleton-Century)—a book highly to be recommended to those interested in reviewing detective stories—reports that "it is a matter of sober statistical record that one out of every four new works of fiction published in the English language belongs to this category, while the devotion the form has managed to arouse in millions of men and women in all walks of life, the humble and the eminent, has become a latter-day legend."

Mr. Haycraft, who long has been interested in this subject, comments on the "increasing excellence of detective story reviewing on both sides of the water" and makes these specific suggestions:

". . . The first and greatest requirement of the detective story review is that it should never under any circumstances give the plot away. The reasons for this rule would seem sufficiently obvious: yet it *has* been done! It is well, too, that the reviewer should have some knowledge of and liking for this sort of literature. As Chesterton pointed out somewhere, no one would think of handing a book of poetry for review to a critic who dislikes or is indifferent to poetry; and the reviewer who holds a similar position with regard to so specialized a genre as the detective story is equally incapable of producing a useful estimate. . . . The conscientious reviewer will also endeavor to classify each book clearly as to the general division into which it falls, so that those readers whose tastes lie in special directions may be advised or warned, as the case may be. He will similarly state prominently the name of the sleuth and any continuing significant characters, realizing that they will strike a helpful reminiscent note with many readers who do not attempt to keep authors' names in mind. . . ."

As for the appeal of the detective story to so many different types, there are several possible explanations. Some of the psychologists say that problem-solving is a fundamental instinct or tendency, common to all of us. In the detective story, we are constantly trying to beat the author to the solution of the murder or murders. Another appeal is that of vicarious experience. This is mentioned in another connection earlier in this chapter. We can enjoy many exciting thrills in the detective story, with no personal hazards. Escape and "mental relaxation" are yet other possible explanations.

Clifton Fadiman thinks that the chief fascination of the detective story comes about because it supplies a happy ending which adults can accept without shame. This wish for the happy ending is very strong and is a carry-over from childhood, when in reading, and to some extent in life itself, everything worked out well. In the detective story, justice triumphs, evil is punished, boy gets girl, but with a minimum of sticky sentiment. This, Mr. Fadiman thinks, is what Philip Guedalla had in mind when he wrote:

"The detective story is the normal recreation of noble minds."

# X

# POETRY

*In every volume of poems something good may be found.*

—Samuel Johnson.

*Poetry—the best words in their best order.*

—Samuel Taylor Coleridge.

*We hold that the most wonderful and splendid proof of genius is a great poem produced in a civilized age.*

—Thomas Babington Macaulay.

# POETRY

A. E. HOUSMAN in his book, *The Name and Nature of Poetry,* writes:

"A year or two ago, in common with others, I received from America a request that I would define poetry. I replied that I could no more define poetry than a terrier can define a rat, but that I thought we both recognized the object by the symptoms which it provokes in us. Experience has taught me, when I am shaving of a morning, to keep watch over my thoughts, because if a line of poetry strays into my memory, my skin bristles so that the razor ceases to act. This particular symptom is accompanied by a shiver down the spine; there is another which consists in a constriction of the throat and a precipitation of water to the eyes; and there is a third which I can only describe by borrowing a phrase from one of Keats' last letters, where he says, speaking of Fanny Brawne, 'everything that reminds me of her goes through me like a spear.' The seat of this sensation is the pit of the stomach." *

This quotation suggests that poetry is difficult to define. It may also be said that it is a literary form which is difficult to review with the beauty and charm of language that good poetry deserves.

Poetry, said Voltaire, "is the music of the soul; and, above all, of great and feeling souls."

* From *The Name and Nature of Poetry* by A. E. Housman (Cambridge University Press, England). By permission of The Macmillan Company, publishers, U. S.

Poetry, wrote Matthew Arnold, is "simply the most beautiful, impressive, and widely effective mode of saying things."

Robert Frost was once asked to give a poet's definition of poetry. He replied: "A complete poem is one where an emotion has found its thought, and the thought has found the words."

W. Somerset Maugham in one of his novels (*Cakes and Ale*) discourses on poetry in this way:

"The crown of literature is poetry. It is its end and aim. It is the sublimest activity of the human mind. It is the achievement of beauty. The writer of prose can only step aside when the poet passes; he makes the best of us look like a piece of cheese." *

All of these extracts have something in common. They all suggest certain fundamentals of poetry. Poetry, they seem to say, is a form of composition which in whole or in part is articulated in rhythmical language, perhaps metrical, expressing or implying beauty, imagery, lofty thought, aspiration, pathos, grief, despair, tragedy, or similar emotions and sentiments.

Poems may follow the traditional pattern or they may take the free verse form. Manner of expression or subject-matter may be of first importance. Poems may be short, and again they may be written as long narratives. There are no hard and fast rules as to length and form. Some texts and teachers say that the *sonnet* is a poem of fourteen lines written in iambic pentameter with a conventional rhyme scheme. The *ballad* is usually a swiftly moving story, told realistically. An *elegy* is a lament, frequently long and deeply emo-

* From *Cakes and Ale,* by W. Somerset Maugham, Doubleday and Co., Inc.

tional. The *epic* has a wider scope—it narrates and sums up an epoch. The *ode* is the most dignified, the most stately and elaborate poem, and has for its theme only the most dignified of subjects.

In writing about books of poetry, a reviewer may ask such questions as—

*Is this a work of power, originality, individuality?*
*Has the poet expressed beauty, imagery, inspiration?*
*Is he philosophical?*
*Is the thought concrete or abstract?*
*Is it clear?*

The reviewer must determine in his own mind what is the poet's intention, and he must honestly answer whether he thinks the poet has succeeded. He must offer in evidence his reasons for any assertion that he makes. Indeed, he must support every sentence with certainty and with conviction, all the while understanding and trying to deal sympathetically, yet objectively, with the poem.

In reviewing poetry, representative extracts should be quoted. Comparisons may be made with the works of other poets and previous writing by the same author.

In some collected editions of a particular poet's works will be found an interpretative introduction, from which a reviewer may secure helpful ideas, facts, and quotations for his review. In many instances, such an introduction or preface is in itself a review or a scholarly literary appraisal of a poet's work. Some of these are models of varying degrees of excellence for the reviewer.

In reviews of poetry, just as in other types, the reviewer should tell something about the author—his background, his education, and whether or not his poetry is incidental to other writing or even another occupation. William Carlos Williams, for instance, was a physician, and Wallace Stevens was a top executive of an insurance company.

Because of the very personal character of poetry, the biographical note may well be stressed in the review. Much poetry is but the lengthened shadow of the man or woman who wrote it. A review of such work can quite appropriately, therefore, be an essay in personality delineation almost as much as in poetic interpretation.

Prof. Earl Daniels of Colgate University in his *The Art of Reading Poetry* suggests that the beginner in poetic appreciation should read each poem *six* times, as follows:

"1. Read the poem rapidly, *aloud*. This is to get the beginnings of a sense of the whole. Do not bother about details. . . .

"2. Read silently, for detailed understanding. Bring the dictionary and the other volumes of the minimum reference library into play. Make notes; preferably, mark the poem. Read not only line by line, but word by word, and allow nothing of the meaning to escape your scrutiny. . . .

"3. Read silently, for imagery. This calls for special attention to figures of speech, particularly to metaphors and similes. All words should be considered for their picture-suggesting potentialities. . . .

"4. Read silently, paying particular attention to the way the poet has put his poem together, to the organization and structure. Into what major divisions does the poem fall? How are the parts connected? Are they arranged in effective order? Can you see possible improvement of the arrangement? What connections are there between line and stanzaic patterns and the thought-divisions of the poem? Where and how has the poet heightened his meaning by comparison, contrast, irony, or other device.

"5. Read silently and aloud. This time the attention should be centered on technique, on the craftsmanship of the poet. Rime and meter, rightly understood, belong here, with devices like alliteration, and assonance. . . .

"6. Read aloud, in a final, synthetic reading to put together results of all previous readings, so that details may fall into proper places, contributing their part to the effect of the whole. By this time the reader's poem, so far as it is possible for him to make it so, should be pretty much the same in idea and sound as the poem the poet originally wrote.

"To read aloud is a law for reading poetry to which there are no exceptions; too much emphasis cannot be laid upon it. Poetry is always music, and as we should not think of judging a musical composition by examining the black notes printed on a staff, without hearing it played or sung, so we ought never to judge poetry without hearing it. Only those who read aloud, who *hear,* can come to a right enjoyment of poetry. Read aloud to yourself. Those about you may believe you have lost your mind, but the end in view is worthwhile enough to warrant incurring even that suspicion. Anyone who can call words can, with little practice, learn to read aloud well enough to make considerable difference in his feelings about poetry."

After one understands fully the purpose of each of these readings, he can, of course, combine the six into a smaller number of readings.

In his instructive chapter "Reviewing Verse" in *First Principles of Verse,* the distinguished poet and teacher Robert Hillyer writes:*

* From *First Principles of Verse* by Robert Hillyer, The Writer, Inc.

"All critics are agreed that there are three questions to be answered in connection with any work of art: What is the author's purpose? Has he succeeded in it? Is it a creditable purpose? These questions must be answered, directly or indirectly, in every review, because they subject the work under discussion to three sets of standards necessary for a complete appraisal. The first question does justice to the author. It assures a careful reading with a view to establishing the ideas and emotions which the author desired to express. The second question brings to bear the standards of the medium in which the author has expressed himself. These standards are entirely impersonal; they are the results of all experiments that have gone before. The third question returns to the idea or emotion, this time measuring it, not by the author's own standards, but by the standards of humanity. If, after conscientious examination, we cannot answer the first question correctly, then we conclude that the artist is obscure, incomprehensible. If we answer No to the second, then he is not skillful in the style of his art; and if No to the third, then he is an eccentric or a trifler, who has nothing to say worth hearing.

"Let us apply these three questions to poetry.

"The first question is the most difficult to answer in considering a poem, because so frequently the author's purpose is hidden—even from his conscious self. Thus, we must search further than the apparent purpose in order to find the poetical purpose underlying the whole work. If we remember that whereas prose *states,* poetry *suggests,* we shall be more on the alert. We shall then proceed beyond the mere statements of the poem to find the author's purpose in the suggestions.

"Let us take two examples. A careful reading of Holmes's

'The Chambered Nautilus' will show us that every figure and phrase in the poem is devoted to the 'moral' expressed in the last, and the most emphatic, stanza. The purpose here was to paint such pictures as should apply directly to the lesson, 'Build thee more stately mansions, O my soul.'

"We turn to Keats' 'Ode on a Grecian Urn.' Again, at the conclusion of the poem we find a moral:

> *"Beauty is truth, truth beauty,"—that is all*
> *Ye know on earth, and all ye need to know.*

Are we to say, then, that the author's purpose here was also the building up of allegorical pictures? Not if we have read carefully. If we have given ourselves to the poem, we have seen a succession of images, pleasing in themselves; we have felt a certain melancholy, an agreeable melancholy, such as we always feel in the presence of the ephemeral beauty of earth; and we have balanced against this mood the thought that art can give immortality to passing loveliness. Our senses, our emotions, our minds, all are addressed in the polyphony of the 'Ode,' and all are stimulated. Furthermore, the poem is moving, not static. The final development is in the thought, 'Beauty is truth,' and so forth, but this is by no means the purpose of the whole poem, any more than the final chord is the purpose of a symphony. It merely provides a dignified conclusion. Taking all this into consideration, we remark that whereas 'The Chambered Nautilus' is a poem with a moral, the 'Ode on a Grecian Urn' is a poem with a mood. That was the author's purpose: to communicate a mood in which our senses, emotions, and mind should all be involved.

"What is the author's purpose in 'Kubla Khan'? In Landor's 'Past ruin'd Ilion Helen lives'? In Burns's 'A Red, Red Rose'?

"Not all poems, in fact very few poems, are as polyphonic as Keats' 'Ode.' Very often an author will intend to stimulate but one side of our nature. Thus, 'Kubla Khan' has to do only with the senses—by the incantation of the verse and the pictures it presents to the inner eye. Landor's epigram is addressed to the mind; Burns's lyric, to the heart. Of course, all poetry, by its form, must involve the senses to some extent; therefore, we always discover some 'sensuous appeal.' We must distinguish between the sensuous element in the nature of poetry itself and that in the purpose of the author. For example, sensuous appeal plays little part in the satires of Alexander Pope. On the other hand, it is by far the dominant element in the imagistic poems of Amy Lowell.

"Until we have established the exact intention of the poet, we cannot proceed to the next question: Has the poet succeeded in his intention?

"Now we come to all the impersonal standards of the art of poetry. We must consider the phrasing, the metre, the rhythm, the rhyming, the figures of speech, the verbal felicity. What sort of *maker* is this poet? We shall probably have to judge his work, too, by the requirements of different set forms he has employed. Has he written sonnets? We know the rules for the various sonnet forms, and we must discover whether or not he has complied with them. Yet this is not enough. It may be he has broken the rules in several instances. We cannot rush to any verdict of Guilty as soon as we discover that fact. We must decide whether or not he has violated the rules intentionally. Someone has described a gentleman as a man who is never *unintentionally* rude. A good writer very often violates the set rules even of so definitely established a form as the sonnet. Now if he has done so deliberately, we must determine whether or not his deviation from the norm justifies his experiment. For example, it has long been considered bad practice to write an iambic pentameter consisting of ten monosyllables. Pope has made fun of such clumsiness thus:

*And ten low words oft creep in one dull line.*

Very well, there is the rule. Turn to Drayton's sonnet, 'Since there's no help, come, let us kiss and part'—one of the finest poems in this form. Each of the first three lines is made up of ten monosyllables. There are many poets who never broke a rule and yet never composed a memorable line; scarcely any great poet—if, indeed, any at all—has been rule-perfect. Let us not swing to a hasty conclusion that breaking rules is a virtue. By no means. But we must bear in mind that there is a double standard in literature: first, the set rule, which constitutes the norm; second, deviation from the set rule, which heightens the main effect of the poem as a whole. Finally, in considering these matters, we may come to the legitimate conclusion that although the poem, with all its technical faults, is noble, it would be better if the rules had not been broken. But this decision I recommend only to such experts as think they could suggest improvements!

"In connection with this second question, too, we must consider the sensuous element, already referred to, which is inherent in the art of poetry. Are the images merely embellishments, or are they, as they should be, part of the general structure? Is the verse musical? Are we moved by the sound of the words even without trying to understand the meaning?

"The third question, too, requires a broad answer, and with this subject we have dealt before. Was the author's intention creditable? Worth our while? A creditable intention will be to communicate a fine emotion or idea to as large a number of fellow human beings as possible. A poet who desires merely to express his own idiosyncrasies without reference to general human experience is no poet at all, but an exhibitionist. All art is more or less excellent as its intention is more or less communal, so long as it is addressed to the deeper emotions, feelings, and thoughts of the community. A verse writer may win fame and money by publishing sentimental ditties which are vastly popular and yet stimulate only the cheaper minds and hearts. Such a man is negligible. At the other extreme is the egotist who expects the world to be interested in his eccentricities of emotion or thought.

"A lack in the community itself prevents great art from taking hold of the majority of people. Therefore, we must modify our reading of the word communal. The community of poetry is the public which will respond to emotions, sensations, and thoughts expressed in poetic form. As we attempt to define this public, we are forced to become vague because we are at the other end of another puzzling definition, that of poetry itself. What is poetry? Tell me what it is, and I will tell you the sort of person who will respond to it.

"Therefore, we must admit that the correct answering of this third question depends on the critical talent of the answerer. A critic with shallow emotions will aver that Mr. Edgar Guest's intention is excellent. A critic who likes nothing but 'rattling good stories' in verse will certainly have no quarrel with Mr. Robert Service's poetic purpose. A critic who admires only the things that make him laugh, will insist that the intention of all comic verse is thoroughly artistic.

All our prejudices, our tastes, our environment and our heredity are involved when we would answer the third question.

"Practically, what can we do about it? I can give only counsel of perfection. First, read widely, so that even though you cannot define it, you will know the poetic intention when you see it. No one can define life, but everyone can live wisely through experience. You must experience poetry before you can profitably judge it. Secondly, as soon as you deliver an opinion, examine it to make sure no fluff of prejudice or personal irritation is clinging to it. I suggest doing this after giving the opinion, because it is humanly easier to revise an opinion than to suppress it altogether. If you are writing, all you have to do is to use an eraser; if you are talking, you can eat your words. No diet is so strengthening to moral fibre as one's own words. Lastly, if you feel you are not competent to decide whether or not the author's intention is creditable, answer the first two questions as conscientiously as you can, and frankly confess your inability to answer the third. Tell your reader to decide that for himself. He will, anyway, even though you speak with the tongues of angels."

Often, a reviewer will be given a group of books of poetry to review. Here is the way Joseph Bennett, a poet and critic and an editor of *The Hudson Review,* handled this assignment in the New York *Times Book Review:*

COUNTRY WITHOUT MAPS. By Jean Garrigue. 82 pp. New York: The Macmillan Company. $3.95.
THE ASTRONOMERS. By Edgar Bowers. 36 pp. Denver: Alan Swallow. $2.50.

THE LAST HERO. And Other Poems. By Louis Coxe. 101 pp. Nashville: Vanderbilt University Press. $4.
THE CARNIVORE. By David R. Slavitt. 58 pp. Chapel Hill: University of North Carolina Press. $3.50.

In "Pays Perdu," the principal poem of "Country Without Maps," Jean Garrigue has produced a poem whose force, I think, has not been equaled in English in recent years. There are other good poems in the book, but "Pays Perdu" transcends them. For all its 11 pages of close text, it cannot be shortened by a line; this is no "Paterson" pudding. The poem is an eclogue; pastorally it describes a quest through stark landscape on a day of brilliant wind. In the mountains, under the blue of the dry sky, there is a remnant of population. Here is staged an epiphany, in the manner of "Burnt Norton"; here among peaks is the rose garden, the still point.

Everything is right about what Miss Garrigue does; there is no other way. What more can one ask? This talent, however at variance with the current muse of domestic anguish, must be reckoned with. It is a talent that has come up, here, with a major poem, with a beginning, a middle and an end, an achievement the current mode of private confession is unable to accomplish.

I am enthusiastic about much of Edgar Bowers's "The Astronomers." Some of his compressed forms accomplish more in a single poem than many poets do in a lifetime. "The Astronomers of Mont Blanc," the opening sonnet, is a work of power, grandeur and discipline. It is worth more, for example, than all of John Berryman's Pulitzer-winning "77 Dream Songs," though it exists on a different plane of intent and accomplishment. Too strong to be associated with any round-robin clique, it has meaningfulness and precision. The Valéryesque densities of his freighted "Adam's Song to Heaven," his nudging among the blind roots of Christian belief in "An Answer," the stately explicitness of the first poem of "Autumn Shade," these provide an intellectual feast of logical, hard-working language, spare and authoritative. Such poems demonstrate that quality of high seriousness which has faded from poetry in the last 20 years.

Louis Coxe's "The Last Hero" has the overriding quality of dignity; it is honest, sober and sincere, but not old-fashioned. As in his earlier work, Coxe provides eloquent utterance when he enters the age of sail or the age of steam: two superb poems are "Cruising," and the long, fast-paced, exciting, yet elegiac narrative, "The Strait." He seems to have too many "occasions for poems," to "make" too many subjects which do not need poems written about them. He translates Apollinaire well, Baudelaire badly; but otherwise he demonstrates a wide range of professional competence.

David R. Slavitt in "The Carnivore" provides us with history lessons that are obvious and plodding and a collection of conventional European picture postcards. But "The Lemmings," "Financial Statement," "Maquillage" and his first-rate "The Carnivore" are witty, deft and compassionate. On the basis of the skill, the insight and the perfection of his title poem and others, he shows himself to be a poet of inspired present accomplishment, and an exciting future.

# XI

# CHILDREN'S BOOKS

*Child! Do not throw this book about;*
*Refrain from the unholy pleasure*
*Of cutting all the pictures out!*
*Regard it as your choicest treasure.*

—Hilaire Belloc.

*Dear little child, this little book*
*Is less a primer than a key*
*To sunder gates where wonder waits*
*Your "Open Sesame!"*

—Rupert Hughes.

*"What is the use of a book," thought Alice, "without pictures or conversations?"*

—Lewis Carroll.

## CHILDREN'S BOOKS

EXPERTS SAY the genuine literary classics for children currently being used in the classroom stimulate the child's desire to learn to read because the stories themselves have more substance and point. For this reason, with all signs pointing toward increased emphasis on good literature for children, the field of reviewing children's books assumes added significance.

The reviewing of books for children has certain elements in common with the effective reviewing of books in any category.

The review should state clearly the author's purpose in writing the book as well as its central theme. It should explore the value of the book to a given reader. And it should leave no doubt as to the reviewer's considered evaluation of the work.

To these criteria may be added the advice of Joseph Wood Krutch, mentioned elsewhere in this work, that the book reviewer must "not only tell what the book is like, but also manage to recreate in the mind of the reader some approximation to the experience produced in him by the reading of the book itself."

This is especially important to the reviewer of children's books, since his or her purpose usually is to guide a child and/or his parents in the selection of attractive books of some value.

Along with the broader qualities just mentioned, the review of a child's book must include specific data unnecessary to the adult book review, but essential to the younger reader. There should be a statement of age groups for which the work will have interest; e.g., "For Ages 4 to 8," "Ages 7 to 10," "Age 12 and up." This, of course, enables not only the child or his parents to select books wisely and well, but is helpful to those who wish to make a gift to a child not seen frequently. This is often accomplished through the use of headings, others of which may indicate fiction, and non-fiction, or more specialized subject-matter, such as the ones used by the book page in the *National Parent-Teacher Magazine:* "Fairy Tales and Fantasy," "People Who Have Adventures," "Poetry, Rhymes and Music," "History in Fact and Fiction," "Picture Story Books," and "Animal Stories."

Within the body of the article, more specialized information may be used to qualify the book under consideration. For example, a review of *The Sign of the Flying Goose* by George Laycock in *Boys' Life* states that the book is "for Explorers or other young adults bucking for conservation." This briefly and clearly states the range of reader-interest, beyond the simple one of age category.

Basic and standard for reviews of children's books also is the inclusion of the name of the illustrator and the kinds of illustrations used. Since illustrations are an important feature of most juvenile books most book buyers wish to have this information. In such popular children's classics as the Dr. Seuss books, the illustrations are perhaps equally as important as the printed matter. Here is a review by Ruth Hill Viguers from *The Horn Book:*

DRAGON FROM THE NORTH. By Anita Hewett. 32 pp. 10¼" x 7⅛". McGraw 2.50. Library edition 2.63 net.

Illustrated by Gioia Fiammenghi. As the little green Lizard traveled through the forest, news of his coming passed from the Black Swan to the Kangaroo Mouse, to the Kangaroo, to the Cassowary, Bower Bird, Possum, Platypus, Turkey, and Wombat. The rumor spread and grew until Lizard discovered, to his surprise and delight, that he was "a great fierce dragon." Lively drawings—ink line and crayon, with brown and yellowish green added—interpret the folk theme and acquaint children with some amusingly different kinds of animals.

In many modern non-fiction works for children, such as the *Life Magazine* series of authoritative scientific books, excellent photographs and diagrams play an important part. Many publications which have book pages or sections for children reprint selected illustrations from books they review.

In non-fiction works, authorship is significant for two reasons:

First, the author may be a notable figure in his field who has written works on the adult level, producing a simplified version for youthful readers. This fact, if it exists, should be made clear in the review.

Second, the author may have written other works of a similar nature for children. Previous works should be cited in the review, as a valuable guidepost to the child or parent who may be familiar with them.

Related to authorship are authenticity and accuracy of the non-fiction work for children. Therefore, insofar as the reviewer is able, he should check on the background of the author if he is not well known. His qualifications should be examined thoroughly and stated in the review. An example of this careful documentation appears in the "Books for Young People" section of *Saturday Review:*

> *Cortes and the Aztec Conquest.* By the editors of *Horizon Magazine.* Author, Irwin Blacker, Consultant, Gordon Eckholm. Illustrated with paintings and drawings and artifacts of the period. American Heritage-Harper & Row. 153 pp. $3.95. *The French Revolution.* By the editors of *Horizon Magazine.* Consultant, David L. Dowd. American Heritage-Harper & Row. 153 pp. $3.95. Here are two new titles in the Heritage-Horizon series, with many excellent pictures characteristic of the series. *Cortes* is particularly rich in these. The progress of the French Revolution is also shown graphically, though the pictures are closer to us in time and some of them more familiar. Young people.

Admonitions not to give the plot away have been made elsewhere in this book, but should be reiterated here in connection with the reviews of juvenile fiction. However, one of the finest devices for achieving the effect which Mr. Krutch suggests—"recreating an approximation of the experience"—is by beginning the review with a vivid précis of the situation in which the fictional character finds himself. For example, Alice Dalgliesh's review, also in the *Saturday Review,* of a book entitled *Obadiah the Bold* by Brinton Turkle, plunges immediately into the heart of the matter:

"Obadiah Starbuck lived in old Nantucket (where else would a Starbuck live?), and he had a new spyglass, made of brass and very beautiful. He announced that when he grew up he was going to be a pirate. There was, however, a difficulty. 'Has thee ever heard of a Quaker pirate?' asked his brother, Moses. One rainy day the children were making-believe pirate and played a trick on Obadiah, who found he didn't want to be a pirate after all."

This introductory teaser cleverly sets the scene, introduces the characters, and intrigues the prospective reader with the promise of exciting action, all *without* divulging the essence of the story.

Other effective reviews employ different introductory methods, sometimes leading off with statements of the timeliness or topicality which make certain books appropriate to a particular time of year.

Long-winded discussions of a juvenile book's literary merit are unsuitable and unwise. This does not mean, however, that an evaluation of this nature should be omitted entirely. The reviewer's opinion of the work on the basis of effective writing, consistency of purpose, organization, etc., should be made clear, but this can be done in a few well-selected phrases which blend into the general description of the book.

Marjorie Burger, for example, in a review for the "Books for Young Readers" page of the New York *Times Book Review,* says of *The Question Box* by Jay Williams:

"There are elements of wisdom and good sense along with the excitement, and the author arranges his incidents with a refreshing childlike logic and directness that scorn mere adult plausibility."

This one clear-cut sentence is enough to establish the reviewer's high regard for the book.

Many publications which feature reviews of children's books serve mainly as a sort of recommendation service, mentioning only those books which meet certain standards, this being a notable point of difference from reviews of adult literature. However, some use reviews which express unfavorable reaction, such as the one by Barbara Wersba, also in the *Times Book Review,* which ends with the comment:

"Alas, it is all too slapdash and casual; strung together like a comic strip. There is nothing more entertaining than science-fiction when it makes fictional sense. When it doesn't, one is quickly disenchanted."

Distinction should be made between the children's book section which serves merely as a catalogue of new juvenile literature, with brief factual descriptions of the works, and that which definitely evaluates the books according to their merits. The decision as to which course to follow is naturally up to the editor of the publication, but it is certainly best to stick to one or the other after the decision is made. Those reviews which are known to be read primarily by the parents rather than the children would be more likely to analyze a book in depth, since children are more concerned with information about the story-content than with a learned evaluation.

This review, from *Parents' Magazine,* shows, through its use of adult vocabulary, and perhaps too-complete resume of the plot, that it was written for adult, rather than juvenile consumption:

"*Nail Soup,* retold by Harve Zemach. Illustrated by Margo Zemach. Follett, $2.50. This is a retelling of an amusing old Swedish tale about a hungry tramp and a greedy old woman. The tramp boasts that he can make soup with a nail, and ingeniously and slyly persuades the stingy old woman to add barley, potatoes, meat, flour, and milk to the nail and boiling water. The comic illustrations contribute fun to the appealing story. (5-8)"

Obviously written for the young reader himself is a review from "Book Corner" of *Child Life*. The language is appropriate for the age-group (about 6 to 10 years), when one considers both reading capability and comprehension. It employs the topicality of the Christmas season, and uses a technique designed to excite the interest of the child:

*The Second Christmas* by Louis Untermeyer
Hallmark Cards, Inc. $2.50

What happened on the second Christmas? Everyone knows the story of the first Christmas, but what was the Christ Child's first birthday like? After the Holy Family fled to Egypt, they lived in fear and awaited a time when it would be safe to return to Nazareth. A sign as unexpected as it is welcome provides them with a second Christmas almost as joyful as the first! This book contains a dozen oil paintings by Louis Marek which add to its beauty. Readers of all ages will thrill to Mr. Untermeyer's story.

Important in book reviewing for children is the careful matching of the type of book selected for review to the readership of the publication in the case of specialized periodicals. *Boys' Life*, the official magazine of the Boy Scouts of America, and *American Girl*, the Girl Scouts' publication, are good examples of highly specialized groups. In keeping with the tastes of the audiences they serve, book reviewers for these magazines select books with a sure appeal. A recent issue of *Boys' Life* reviewed the following, all with a definite interest for boys aged 10 to 15: *The Most Beautiful Place* by Gina Ruck-Pauquet, a story of a homeless boy and his pet donkey; *Boys' Life Book of World War Two Stories;*

*The Sign of the Flying Goose* by George Laycock, a book concerning the National Wildlife Refuge System; *Teen-Age Fitness* by Bonnie Prudden; *Here Is Your Hobby: Skiing* by William O. Foss; *Islands in the Sky* by Arthur C. Clarke, a science-fiction story; and *Prayers for Scouts* by Walter Dudley Calvert.

Breezy language, matter-of-fact but colorful, characterizes these reviews for an audience of boys. This, for example:

"This book hit me such a wallop that, when I finished the last chapter, I got up and went out to where my old dog was sleeping and begged it not to die, because I didn't think I could be as brave as Joschko was about his donkey."

*American Girl* reviews books which feature the first romance, mystery, and the "career" stories so popular with teen-age girls. Often it reviews the book forms of continued novels which have appeared first in the magazine. This publication, too, uses an informal style appropriate to its readership. Following is a review from this magazine by Marjorie Vetter:

*High and Haunted Island*. By Nan Chauncey. W. W. Norton, $3.50. If you are looking for a dash of mystery and adventure to brighten your life, we heartily recommend this latest book by a prizewinning Australian author. Much of the story takes place during the best vacation Rusty Ironn and Otter Roxtell had ever enjoyed, when they were permitted to take a hand in sailing the beautiful yacht *Timmari* around the lonely, dangerous waters of the Tasmanian Islands. From the beginning of the cruise there were strangely puzzling circumstances in the behavior of Otter's father and a seaman named Jake. Why did Mr. Roxtell suddenly change his mind and join the cruise only when Port Davey was mentioned? What was back of Jake's strange behavior? Who carved Otter's initials on a tree at Port Davey? Years earlier, during the War, two young schoolgirls, going home for the holidays, had been put ashore from a steamer threatened by an enemy raider on the wild, uninhabited island of Port Davey. Could the two young girls find enough to eat to keep them alive as days passed and the steamer did not return? Could they survive the biting cold of the long nights? What happened to them is a colorful and intriguing chapter in itself. You will find it and the answers to all these questions in this unusual tale of excitement and suspense in a remote spot, vividly portrayed.

Among the most important publications reviewing books for children are the *ALA Bulletin*, the *School Library Journal* and the useful magazine, *The Horn Book* which is devoted entirely to children's books and reading. Anyone reviewing books for children should be familiar with these publications.

One last word of advice to the writer of children's book reviews concerns a common pitfall—that of the overworked adjective. When adults are faced with describing a book for children they all too often fall back on a sort of patronizing vocabulary containing five or six adjectives which almost always begin with "charming," work their way through "delightful" and "appealing," ultimately reaching "whimsical" and "refreshing." There are more concrete and effective ways to describe a book of which one really approves. A Roget's *Thesaurus* or similar work will prove helpful in this and other connections.

Summing up the key factors to be remembered for reviewing children's books, the following decalogue is offered for use as a check list to apply both before and after the review is written:

1. State, directly or by implication, the author's purpose and the book's central theme.
2. Indicate the ages and/or interest group for which the book is intended.
3. Give the essential information about the author.
4. Evaluate the book's worth for the reader.
5. Try to evoke in the reader of the review an image of the experience he will have in reading the book.
6. Describe the type or types of illustrations used, naming the illustrator, and mention his or her qualifications.
7. Comment on the authenticity of facts or background information.
8. Make literary criticism brief but explicit.
9. Taking into account the readers for which the review is being written, choose language and set the tone accordingly.
10. Avoid the cliches common to descriptions of children's literature.

# XII

# BOOK TITLES

*Unlike my subject now shall be my song;*
*It shall be witty, and it sha'n't be long.*

—Philip Dormer Stanhope,
Earl of Chesterfield.

*Of all my verse, like not a single line;*
*But like my title, for it is not mine.*
*That title from a better man*
*I stole;*
*Ah, how much better, had*
*I stol'n the whole!*

—Robert Louis Stevenson.

## BOOK TITLES

REVIEWERS should remember that sometimes there is a little story—worth a sentence or more—in the origin of the title of a book.

When Medora Field Perkerson's *Blood on Her Shoe* was fresh off the press, for example, so many readers inquired about the title that the publishers issued a news release saying it came from the Cinderella legend. When the cruel sisters cut off a bit of heel or toe, hoping to wear the glass slipper, the Prince was warned of their perfidy by Cinderella's pet pigeons. "There's blood on her shoe—not the right bride for you."

Book titles are generally of four types:

(1) Those that are merely labels—descriptive of the book.

(2) Those that have some kind of literary background—extracts from various sources.

(3) Those that are associated in some way with the origin and development of a book—how the author got the idea for the book or some incident in the development of the script.

(4) Those that are what advertising men would call "teaser" heads—titles that are designed to arouse the curiosity rather than to describe the book (although some are descriptive).

Titles in the first category range all the way from simple brief labels, such as *The Henry James Reader* edited by

Leon Edel or *Kennedy* by Theodore C. Sorensen to long, and sometimes quaint, descriptions such as *Fifty Years—Being a Retrospective Collection of Novels, Novellas, Tales, Drama, Poetry and Reportage and Essays (Whether Literary, Musical, Contemplative, Historical, Biographical, Argumentative or Gastronomical) All Drawn from Volumes Issued during the Last Half-Century by Alfred & Blanche Knopf, The Whole Selected, Assembled and Edited, with an Introduction and Sundry Commentaries* by Clifton Fadiman or *Verse by the Side of the Road, the Story of the Burma Shave Signs* by Frank Rowsome, Jr. These longer titles are suggestive of the names of some of the earlier magazines, the first two of which in this country were Andrew Bradford's *American Magazine or a Monthly View of the State of the British Colonies*, and Benjamin Franklin's *General Magazine, and Historical Chronicle, for All the British Plantations in America.*

From the point of view of the reviewer, the most interesting titles—those that lend themselves best to comment by the reviewer—are those in Categories 2, 3, and 4. The literary background of titles is always of interest—so much so that the greater part of this chapter will be devoted to examples of this particular theme.

Stark Young's *So Red the Rose* comes from Omar Khayyám's *Rubáiyát:*

> *"I sometimes think that never blows so red*
> *The rose as where some buried Caesar bled."*

Howard Spring's *My Son, My Son* is from David's lament over Absalom (II *Samuel* 18:33):

> *". . . O my son Absalom! my son, my son Absalom! would God I had died for thee, O Absalom, my son, my son!"*

Edna Ferber's *A Peculiar Treasure* derives from *Exodus* 19:5: "Now therefore, if ye will obey my voice indeed, and keep my covenant, then ye shall be a peculiar treasure unto me above all people: for all the earth is mine: and ye shall be unto me a kingdom of priests, and an holy nation."

Other titles that come from the Bible are *Keepers of the House,* the 1965 Pulitzer Prize novel by Shirley Ann Grau (*Ecclesiastes* 12:3), *My Brother's Keeper* by Marcia Davenport (*Genesis* 4:9—"Am I my brother's keeper?"), *Giants in the Earth* by O. E. Rölvaag (*Genesis* 6:4—"There were giants in the earth in those days"), and *Eastward in Eden* by David Garth (*Genesis* 2:8—"And the Lord God planted a garden eastward in Eden") *The Sun Also Rises* by Ernest Hemingway (*Ecclesiastes* 1:5), *There Shall Be No Night,* the Pulitzer Prize play, by Robert E. Sherwood (*Revelation* 22:5) plus many titles from *The Song of Solomon—The Voice of the Turtle* by John van Druten, *The Little Foxes* by Lillian Hellman, *Comfort Me With Apples* by Peter DeVries, etc.

John Steinbeck's *East of Eden* was taken from the Biblical phrase, while his *The Winter of Our Discontent* is from Shakespeare's *Richard III,* which opens, "Now is the winter of our discontent/Made glorious summer by this sun of York," and his *Of Mice and Men* is a part of Burns' "The best laid plans of mice and men aft gang agley." His *Grapes of Wrath* (Pulitzer Prize novel) is a part of Julia Ward Howe's *Battle Hymn of the Republic:*

*"Mine eyes have seen the glory of the*
*coming of the Lord;*
*He is trampling out the vintage where*
*the grapes of wrath are stored."*

Margaret Mitchell's *Gone with the Wind* is a part of Ernest Dowson's *Non Sum Qualis Eram,* which reads:

*"I have forgot much, Cynara! gone with*
*the wind,*
*Flung roses, roses riotously with the*
*throng,*
*Dancing, to put thy pale, lost lilies out*
*of mind;*
*But I was desolate and sick of an old*
*passion,*
*Yea, all the time, because the dance was*
*long;*
*I have been faithful to thee, Cynara! in*
*my fashion."*

Ernest Hemingway's *For Whom the Bell Tolls* is a part of a paragraph by the philosopher and poet, John Donne:

"No man is an island, entire of itself; every man is a piece of the continent, a part of the mainland; if a clod be washed away by the sea, Europe is the less, as well as if a promontorie were washed away . . . any man's death diminishes me, because I am involved in mankind; and, therefore, never send to know for whom the bell tolls; it tolls for thee."

Eric Knight took his inspiration for *This Above All* from Shakespeare's *Hamlet,* Act 1, Scene 3:

*"This above all: to thine own self be true,*
*And it must follow, as the night the day,*
*Thou canst not then be false to any man."*

The title of Aldous Huxley's *Time Must Have a Stop* is another of Shakespearean origin—*Henry IV* (Part 1), Act 5, Scene 4:

*"But thought's the slave of life, and life time's fool;*
*And time, that takes survey of all the world,*
*Must have a stop."*

Philip Barry's *Tomorrow and Tomorrow* is, of course, from Shakespeare (*Macbeth,* Act 5, Scene 5), as is William Faulkner's *The Sound and the Fury.*

Thornton Wilder's *Heaven's My Destination* should recall the lines that many, as children, have inscribed in their copy books:

*"Johnny Jones is my name,*
*America's my nation,*
*Macon is my dwelling place*
*And Heaven's my destination."*

Granville Hicks' novel, *Only One Storm,* gets its title from an old New England saying:

"There's only been one storm that never cleared up—and that's this one."

George Meredith seems to be the inspiration for many writers. Rosamond Lehmann's *Dusty Answer* is taken from Meredith's *Modern Love:*

*"Ah, what a dusty answer gets the soul*
*When hot for certainties in this our life!"*

Vardis Fisher named four of his novels—*No Villain Need Be, Passions Spin the Plot, We Are Betrayed,* and *In Tragic Life*—from the following from Meredith's *Modern Love:*

*". . . in tragic life, God wot,*
*No villain need be! Passions spin the plot;*
*We are betrayed by what is false within."*

Wallace Stegner's *On a Darkling Plain* is from *Dover Beach* by Matthew Arnold:

*"And we are here as on a darkling plain*
*Swept with confused alarms of struggle and flight*
*Where ignorant armies clash by night."*

The F.P.A. (Franklin P. Adams) book, *Nods and Becks*—in both the title and nature of content—was suggested by these lines from John Milton's *L'Allegro:*

*"Haste thee, Nymph, and bring with thee*
*Jest and youthful Jollity,*
*Quips and Cranks and wanton Wiles,*
*Nods and Becks and wreathed Smiles."*

Burges Johnson's *As Much As I Dare: A Personal Recollection,* derives from these lines of Montaigne:

"I speak truth, not as much as I would, but as much as I dare. And I dare a little more as I grow older."

The title of Vaughan Wilkins' novel *Being Met Together*

is taken from the phrase interpolated by Winston Churchill in the preamble of the Atlantic Charter—"The President of the United States and the Prime Minister, Mr. Churchill, representing His Majesty's Government in the United Kingdom, being met together, deem it right to make known certain common principles in the national policies of their respective countries on which they base their hopes for a better future for the world."

The collection of essays by John Crowe Ransom, Donald Davidson, and other spokesmen of the so-called "agrarian movement" bears the title *I'll Take My Stand,* which, of course, is a part of Daniel Decatur Emmett's song, *Dixie:*

> *"In Dixie land, I'll take my stand,*
> *To lib an' die in Dixie.*
> *Away, away*
> *Away down South in Dixie."*

As for titles that are associated with the origin or production of the book, the following are illustrative:

Cecil Roberts secured the title for his novel, *One Small Candle,* in this way: On the day Mr. Roberts left England for a lecture tour in America, he saw on the roadside near his cottage a new memorial stone which had been erected in memory of a pet dog killed by an automobile. The inscription so impressed Mr. Roberts that it lingered in his mind. "There is not enough darkness in all the world to put out the light of one small candle." In blacked-out Europe, it rang like a challenge; and is a most fitting title for the story he tells of a love and a faith that could not be extinguished.

Temple Bailey's novel, *Red Fruit,* got its title thus:

"The title, *Red Fruit,* came to me in an old orchard in

Maryland, as I watched the loading of great baskets of apples to be sent to the men overseas. There is more, however, than the red fruit of the orchard in this story—there is the red fruit of war, and as my hero, Kim, back from the Pacific, salutes his beloved homeland, the contrast is before him: the orchard, life-giving; the fruit of war, death-dealing."

Edward W. Beattie, Jr., then United Press foreign correspondent, chose the title of *Freely to Pass* from the preamble of his American passport—a document which, in his case, grew from five to ninety-two pages in less than a decade.

Illustrative of "teaser" titles would be *Yes I Can* by Sammy Davis Jr., *The Hater's Handbook* by Joseph Rosner, *There Goes What's Her Name* by Virginia Graham, *The Kandy-Kolored Tangerine-Flake Streamline Baby* by Tom Wolfe, *Anti-Woo* by Stephen Potter, *Crazy Like a Fox* by S. J. Perelman, and Anita Loos' two best sellers, *Gentlemen Prefer Blondes* and *But Gentlemen Marry Brunettes*.

Many more little stories of book titles could be cited. These should suffice, however, to illustrate the point that the origin of book titles, individually and collectively, is usually of interest and may well be borne in mind by reviewers.

# XIII

# WHAT THE EXPERTS SAY

*Literature is the greatest of all sources of refined pleasure, and one of the great uses of a liberal education is to enable us to enjoy that pleasure.*

—Thomas Henry Huxley.

*There is no heroic poem in the world but is at bottom a biography, the life of a man; also, it may be said, there is no life of a man, faithfully recorded, but is a heroic poem of its sort, rhymed or unrhymed.*

—Thomas Carlyle.

## WHAT THE EXPERTS SAY

THE PROOF of the pudding lies in the eating. Applying this platitude to the realm of book reviewing, there should be no better guide to good reviews than the opinions of those who have attained the heights among contemporary critics. In other words, what nuggets of wisdom have the more experienced book reviewers to offer? Here are a few—and it will be noted that all say about the same thing, but in different ways.

J. Donald Adams, while editor of the New York *Times Book Review,* summarized the requirements of that excellent publication thus:

"It seems to me that a good book review, for whatever audience it may be intended, should do three things. It should, first of all, make clear what the author of the book attempted to do; it should convey to the book's potential reader an adequate idea of what the book has to offer him; and it should leave with the reader of the review a definite impression concerning the reviewer's judgment as to the book's quality. I think these three requirements are the most broadly essential. Of course, there are others which are more intangible or which are applicable only in certain instances. Certain books require a greater degree of expository treatment than others; sometimes everything lies in the reviewer's ability to convey the peculiar flavor or quality of a book. In the best reviewing, the reviewer brings to his work something of his own; sometimes factual knowledge, sometimes the capacity of sympathetic understanding."

Edward Weeks, distinguished editor of *The Atlantic Monthly,* who handles the more important reviews for his magazine under the heading, "The Peripatetic Reviewer," discourses on book reviewing with the charm that characterizes all his writing in this way:

"Let me present you with the ten commandments for book reviewers: (1) Don't use loose words—'thrilling,' 'intriguing,' 'cute,' 'grand,' 'swell,'—in talking or writing of books. There are some readers who don't know any better; you do. (2) Practice humility in stating your opinion of a book. Allow for the possibility that your judgment may not be infallible. (3) Don't give away the contents, or the plot, of the book you are discussing. The author has taken a year to prepare its entertainment and surprise. You have absolutely no right to give the show away in three desiccated paragraphs. (4) Read the book: don't skim it. (5) When you read, allow 60 per cent of your thoughts to be swept into the main current of the story: keep the other 40 per cent detached and observant on the river bank. Pause whenever a note seems worth taking. (6) In conclusion, ask yourself what the author is trying to do. (7) Ask yourself how well he has done it. (8) Ask yourself—in your opinion—was it worth doing. (9) If possible, hold what you have written for twenty-four hours and show it to someone whose judgment you respect. Second thoughts will often modify the first flush of enthusiasm. (10) Avoid superlatives: a Shakespeare, a Keats, a Kipling, or a Galsworthy does not reproduce himself every ten years."

Richard Kluger, editor of *Book Week* (a Sunday supplement of book reviews distributed by the New York *Herald*

*Tribune,* Washington *Post,* Chicago *Sun-Times,* etc.) recently explained:

"One thing *Book Week* asks of its reviewers—perhaps the most important thing—is candor. We want them to say, in as engaging a fashion as possible under the circumstances, just how good or bad they think the book is that they are reviewing—and why. It gives the editors of *Book Week* no pleasure to run a sharply negative review of a book that, after all, consumed a great deal or a lot of people's energy and time. It does give us pleasure, on the other hand, to run glowing notices of a deserving book, since all of us—the entire literate community—are enriched by the arrival of a provocative or moving or deeply insightful new work. We are not always sure, of course, if a book deserves the praise (or rebuke) it receives from a reviewer; after all, we rarely have the chance to read in its entirety a book under review before the review arrives. And even then, we neither ask nor expect our reviewer's verdict to agree with ours. In the long run, though, we rely on people whose judgment we have confidence in."

In a statement prepared especially for this book, Harry Hansen (a literary editor of the New York *World-Telegram*) summed up his views on reviewing thus:

"The man who reviews books for a newspaper must know that he cannot use its precious space to address a small coterie of his own or argue the claims of one school of writing. He must interest as many readers as possible in the important and valuable books of the hour, not forgetting that many in his large audience are interested in getting entertainment, information and cultural guidance, and that the number of those familiar with special phases of criticism or able to use an academic jargon is relatively small.

"This does not mean that the reviewer must 'write down' to anyone, but that he must be lucid, understandable, and open-minded. His reviews ought to be timely and keep step with current publications. They ought to be sufficiently expository for the reader to get a clear idea of the contents of the book under discussion. The subjective review, in which the reviewer is more interested in his own views than in the book that is the excuse for his writing, has its place as a newspaper feature, but misses its aim if the reader gets no clear idea of what the author has been trying to say. The opposite extreme is the colorless description of a new book that we find in many newspaper reviews. These reviews are chiefly reporting; they are not written from a point of view and they do not tell where the book stands with relation to others in its field.

"The general reviewer is not likely to be an authority in more than one field, but his wide reading makes him familiar with books of other subjects than his own. It is sometimes argued that only the specialist can accurately judge the books in his field, and this is true so far as final judgment is concerned. But the specialist is not always ready to address an audience that has no preparation in his subject. The general reviewer's opinion is not final, but he ought to be able to present the scope and purpose of a work to readers who, like himself, are eager to be informed.

"With these limitations of medium in mind, the reviewer ought to develop his own method of presenting his opinions. He should not be bound by rules and traditions; his vocabulary is his own and his manner may change from day to day. He is more of an essayist than a reporter, but an essayist who has learned a great deal from the reporter's way of getting at the core of things, losing no time in desultory talk, and making himself clearly understood."

Diana Trilling, book columnist and reviewer for many magazines and newspapers, commented:*

"I think the first responsibility of the critic is to the book, to the object as it really is. I hate reviewing which is primarily directed to the glorification of the reviewer at the expense of the object under examination.

"Of course, we all do show ourselves off when we review a book. It would be a pretty dull affair if we didn't. But there is a considerable difference between using a book one is reviewing as an occasion for speculation and excursion or even perhaps for self-definition and using it for doing one's own private dance on the author's grave. Obviously the critic brings himself to any estimate of a book; but the book makes the objective context within which he works, and he must respect this context even if he despises it."

Orville Prescott, co-editor of "Books of the Times" in the daily New York *Times,* subscribes to a belief which has been expounded earlier in this book, viz., that there is an important difference in the point of view and methods of the critic and the reviewer. He also feels that reviewers are under greater obligation to their readers than to the authors of the books about which they write. He advocates what he calls "violence in reviewing"—a view which will not be shared by those who hold that the weaknesses of a book can be cited or implied without necessarily being brutally unkind to the author. As Aldous Huxley has said, a bad book may come as sincerely from the author's soul as a good one, or, as Cer-

* In an interview in *Counterpoint,* compiled and edited by Roy Newquist, Rand McNally & Co.

vantes once wrote, "nothing can be more impossible than to compose (a book) that may secure the approbation of every reader."

Such statements as these bring up, of course, the ethical considerations in the critic-reviewer's dual obligations—to his readers and to his authors—not to mention publishers, literary agents, and all others who have a part in the conception and birth of a book. Mr. Prescott has some stimulating views on this theme as follows:

"There are as many ways of reviewing or criticizing books as there are reviewers and critics. And there are even more misconceptions of the reviewer's job, some of them no less fantastic than that of my small son who said last week: 'When I grow up I want to be a book reviewer like Daddy and sit down all day and read books.'

"Perhaps we should distinguish first between a *critic* and a *reviewer*. The distinction may be a fine one, almost as imaginary a line as the equator, but it is there. We might say that the critic is usually a professor at a college or university or a contributor to a learned journal, a scholarly quarterly or occasionally to more popular review media. He writes his criticism in comparative leisure, about books that are assigned him or which he has chosen because they are appropriate to his special subject of study. The critic is apt to make detailed analysis of literary techniques and to try to evaluate books in a framework of world literature according to certain standards which he spends much of his life debating. Such critics perform an important function; they often champion particular sides in literary battles and they often shed much light on contemporary culture.

"But a reviewer, at least a daily newspaper reviewer, has a different task. Deluged with floods of books, all of them masterpieces according to their jackets, he must select a few for notice and decide what he is going to do about them. I believe that a newspaper book reviewer should not be concerned with 'constructive criticism' for the author's sake; nor should he indulge in misguided enthusiasm for publishers', authors' and booksellers' sakes. His primary duty is to the readers of his column. He must serve as a guide among the bewildering profusion of new titles; he must act as a sieve sorting out chaff from grain. Books are news, and he must tell his readers about them. He must describe them, state what the author attempted to do, and how well he succeeded in his attempt. So he frequently says that a book is good, or successful, although it is not the kind he himself prefers. But if he has described the book well, his readers should know that it is good of the kind just pointed out. But it may not be good for them.

"People forget this. They forget that book reviews are not supposed to make up somebody else's mind. They are supposed to help him make up his own mind as to whether a book is for him or not. So the reviewer should indicate the author's manner of writing, his general point of view, the theme of his book, the impression it creates. If it is fiction, he should describe the type of characters; but never on pain of excommunication should he outline a plot. If the book is non-fiction, he should present the author's credentials, mention his method and skill or lack of it as a writer, and state his principal thesis. You can give away the point of a detective story, but you do not damage a work of non-fiction by saying what the author thinks should be done to the Germans or what he thinks of Sidney Hillman. These are matters readers need to know.

"Which books should we review? Someone will always be

hurt by omissions no matter which we choose. But three points are my own guideposts:

"1) The importance of the subject here and now at this stage of world history. This means war correspondents' books, books on Germany, Russia, Japan, China, and India, books on politics and economics. The general reviewer, by definition a non-specialist, cannot be an authority on many such matters. He does his best within his own beliefs and prejudices, as impartially as he can.

"2) The second reason why a book is chosen for review is its probable literary merit. If it is the work of a writer of proven ability, if after a judicious sampling it seems promising, if its publishers seem convinced that it is good and not just that it is saleable (you can detect the difference almost by smelling the jacket).

"3) The third reason for choice is books that I hope will interest me personally. If no other deciding factor is present, there is no sense in my doing a book on antique furniture if it bores me stiff when I could do one on breeding Belgian hares if that would fascinate me. If you watch a reviewer for a while you can soon see his tastes.

"A reviewer must watch that he does not overlook good books by unknown writers. He must learn to ignore abusive letters and to discount flattering ones. And above all, he must always be interested. Each new book must be exciting; each day's batch of new books must seem like Christmas. If books began to bore a reviewer, he would soon end up in an asylum. He must always feel that books are important, that they are vital to our culture and to our liberties, that they are the greatest of arts and the finest of entertainments.

"And a reviewer must be blunt. A wretched book must not be let down gently. I believe in violence in reviewing; only with violence can you be of much use to your readers. Mistaken kindness to an author may be a betrayal of your readers. And last of all, valuable newspaper space must not be wasted on a dull book. The reviewer has to try his desperate best to be interesting no matter how dull the book. Sometimes he can't be, of course. But he tries so hard he becomes wan and haggard and gets a hunted look in his eyes. That's why he neglects his wife, abuses his children, and ages prematurely."

David Boroff, a frequent reviewer for the New York *Times* and *Saturday Review,* pointed out:

"A distinction should be made at the outset between book reviewers and critics. The book reviewer works under the gun, so to speak. He gets the book and has only some perfunctory advance notice about it—a press release, perhaps, or a short paragraph describing it in *Publishers' Weekly*. Under pressure for time, he must—in six or seven hundred words—make a judgment about the book as well as give the reader some sense of what the book is about. It is the latter element—the synopsis—that highbrow critics find so distasteful. But it is a responsibility that the book reviewer can hardly avoid. In effect, he is a kind of literary reporter for the general reader. In these respects, he is like the play reviewer, another literary journeyman it is now fashionable to despise.

"The critic, on the other hand, is the strategist in the rear echelons. He is favored by the fact that the smoke of battle has cleared. The worth of the book he is evaluating has begun to crystallize. He can comfortably forgo the bread and butter synopsis and assume that his readers have previously read the reviews. He can, therefore, write in a more leisurely fashion—quarterlies make no effort to review books on time

—and even make ultimate judgments if he is so inclined. But it is precisely this fact—the sober second look—that makes highbrow critics strain a little. If they don't upset the book reviewers' apple cart, then what function do they have?"

In summing up his discussion, Mr. Boroff stated:

"At the risk of Philistinism, I am prepared to acknowledge that when I review a book my hypothetical reader is not one of my academic or literary colleagues—he hardly needs *my* guidance—but rather an engineer in Oneonta, an accountant in Des Moines, a young mother who majored in English and is now at home with three little children. The book reviewer's job is to inform, guide and stimulate all people interested in books. How well the reviewer discharges this function is another matter, but the job itself seems eminently worth doing."

To the problems of reviewing, Joseph Wood Krutch brings experience in both literature and drama, two closely related fields. At one time dramatic editor of *The Nation,* he has also written many book reviews, has taught journalism and dramatic literature at Columbia University for many years, and is the author and editor of a long list of important books. He too stresses a recurring note in this and other chapters—the differences between book reviewing and literary criticism. They are not the same, he insists, and "their aims, problems, and excellences are fundamentally different." Mr. Krutch makes the often overlooked and very excellent point that "the best review is not the one which is trying to be something else." In a development of this theme he said in part:

"In certain technical respects a good review is more difficult to write than a critical essay, because the writer of it must assume a larger number of specific responsibilities. The critical essay is, for instance, not compelled to aim at any particular degree of completeness. It does not have to describe the work under discussion because it may assume that the reader is already familiar with that work and it may also confine itself to whatever aspects of the work it chooses to deal with. The book review, on the other hand, must assume that the reader is not yet familiar with the book under discussion and before the reviewer pronounces any judgment upon it he must put that reader in possession of the facts necessary to make the judgment intelligible. And having done that he must consider the book as a whole, not merely some aspect of it which happens to interest him.

"Within very brief space a satisfactory review must do three quite separate things. It must describe the work being reviewed, it must communicate something of its quality, and it must pass some sort of judgment upon it. Each of these things is quite different from the others but each is necessary.

"Adequate description implies a simple account of the scope and contents of the book and its presence guarantees that the reader will not be left wondering, as he sometimes is, what, in the simplest terms, the book is about. *Communication of quality* implies on the other hand that, in addition to description, the reviewer must provide on a small scale a specimen of what is called impressionistic criticism. He must, that is to say, not only tell what the book is like but also manage to re-create in the mind of his reader some approximation to the experience produced in him by the reading of the book itself. Unless he succeeds in doing that the review cannot become what it is supposed to be—namely, not merely an account of the book on the one hand, nor an independent piece of criticism on the other, but a brief essay which includes within itself all that is necessary to make whatever judgment it may pronounce comprehensible and significant.

"It is not easy to do the three things enumerated in the space of a thousand words or so, and to combine them in such a way as to make them seem not three separate things, but an organic whole. How many reviewers of novels, for instance, seem to know how much of a particular story has to be told in order to form an adequate basis for their impressionistic criticism? And if it is decided that some part of the story must be told, how many know, as a story teller must, whether the incidents will stand by themselves or must be introduced by some comment which creates interest. Yet a first-rate review, despite its miniature scale, raises the same problems as long narratives or expositions raise and they must be solved with skill.

"Doubtless the finest reviewer can hardly hope to have his art fully appreciated by the public. But there is every reason why he should respect it himself. And if he did so he might be less likely either to treat reviewing as a casual affair or be always seeking an opportunity to do something else under the guise of a book review. He might be happier and make his readers happier also if he would take the trouble to ask what a review *qua* review ought to be and if he would ask himself how good, by those standards, anything he has just written really is. His business is not to show how clever he is, or how much he knows, or how well he could write literary criticism on some more exalted level if only he had a chance. His business is to demonstrate how well he can give a reader what that reader has a right to expect from a review."

Since the advent of radio and television, there has been an increasing use of book reviews by these media. Since such reviews first have to be written before they are aired, it is appropriate to include the suggestions of one who is outstanding in this phase of book reviewing—Elmo Ellis, general manager, WSB Radio, Atlanta, co-author with Leonard Reinsch of *Radio Station Management*.

Mr. Ellis, whose reviews are among the best on the air (or in printed media), says:

"I would list the following points as cardinal:

"1. Reading, understanding and developing an opinion of the book—these are the difficult steps. Once these have been mastered, I find that the writing and reading of the review on the air are comparatively simple.

"2. I try, after digesting a book, to determine what is pertinent about it. I ask myself what the volume offers that should be meaningful to my listeners, and how can I best convey the content and spirit of the book? Sometimes I may decide to abstract the entire book. At other times I feel that it is more effective to deal with one facet of a particular book. At any rate, I end up approaching the review with a premise or theme in mind, and the development of the review follows the basic concept on which I have decided.

"3. I strive for simplicity in writing each review. While I do not avoid multi-syllable words, I am always conscious of the fact that the short word is easier to understand than the long word, and the simple sentence is easier to comprehend than the complex one. I try to convey the details a thought at a time, in a conversational manner. I do not deal in a great many names of characters, places or events because the listener cannot absorb a concentration of facts or details in a brief period of time. Instead I try to catch the mood of the book through delineation of a simple story line, or in the case of a non-fiction book, by liberal use of colorful anecdotes and episodes that illustrate the spirit and purpose of the work.

"4. Rarely do I review books that I consider inferior works. If I feel that a book does not deserve a review, then it is questionable, in my mind, whether I should take my time, or the time of the listener, in dealing with it. This does not mean that I hesitate to criticize weaknesses in books that I do review, but I try to choose a worthy volume for each review.

"5. Every author has a purpose in writing a book. His success in achieving his goal depends on both his communicative skills, and on the receptiveness of his readers. I feel a responsibility, as a reviewer, to attempt to understand the author's purpose, to evaluate it, and to convey my findings to the listener. My approach is not to be didactic nor to deal in pedantry, but merely to sketch the volume in a concise manner, extract the essence of its message, provide an evaluation, and then leave it to the individual listener to decide if he has been enticed into reading the book."

# XIV

# SUGGESTED REFERENCES FOR REVIEWERS

*Dictionaries are like watches; the worst is better than none, and the best cannot be expected to be quite true.*

*Knowledge is of two kinds: we know a subject ourselves, or we know where we can find information on it.*

—Samuel Johnson.

## SUGGESTED REFERENCES FOR REVIEWERS

THERE ARE, of course, many textbooks on literary criticism and appreciation. Readers of this handbook have probably encountered some of these in their high school and college courses in English. They certainly may be readily found in almost any library and are listed in many bibliographies. We shall not, therefore, comment on many such texts here.

What are more important for our purposes are the books by publishers, literary agents, and working reviewers. Many of these are informal, all of them are practical, and some of them incorporate the distilled essence of long years of experience in fields closely related to reviewing. These are books which should be read by the reviewer for background. They will give him an inner-sanctum or behind-the-scenes picture of the book world. They will give him the point of view of students of books and their influence.

Reviewers should also be interested in certain technical manuals, such as style books, so several good titles in this category are included.

Books listed in this chapter are essentially of two kinds: (1) those to be read, and (2) those which are in the nature of reference works, and which merit a place on the same shelf with the dictionary. The style manuals and books of synonyms belong in this second category.

The list which follows should be regarded as a suggestive rather than an exhaustive catalogue of reading possibilities for the reviewer. There are, of course, other useful titles already in print, and others will be added from time to time.

Adler, Elmer. *Breaking into Print*. New York: Simon and Schuster.

Contributors are Sherwood Anderson, Robert Benchley, Stephen Vincent Benét, Pearl Buck, A. E. Coppard, Theodore Dreiser, Robinson Jeffers, MacKinlay Kantor, Rockwell Kent, Sinclair Lewis, H. L. Mencken, Christopher Morley, Edwin Arlington Robinson, Edith Wharton, etc. They tell not only how they first got published, but whether they use the typewriter or pen or pencil, how many drafts of an article or story they make before sending the manuscript to the editor, and how many changes they make in proof. The volume is illustrated with facsimile pages of the contributors' manuscripts.

Adler, Mortimer J. *How to Read a Book*. New York: Simon and Schuster.

Described by its author as "a light book about heavy reading . . . a book about reading in relation to life, liberty, and the pursuit of happiness." Dr. Adler has been a professor of the philosphy of law at the University of Chicago, and is now president and director of the Institute of Philosophical Research. He lists the great books of all times, using the famous St. John's College list, as well as those suggested by the University of Chicago, Columbia University, and others.

Bernstein, Theodore M. *The Careful Writer, A Modern Guide to English Usage*. New York: Atheneum.

Copperud, Roy H. *A Dictionary of Usage and Style*. New York: Hawthorn Books.

Evans, Bergen, and Evans, Cornelia. *A Dictionary of Contemporary American Usage.* New York: Random House.

Fowler, H. W. *A Dictionary of Modern English Usage.* (Second Edition revised by Sir Ernest Gowers). New York: Oxford University Press.

Helpful volumes on correct contemporary usage.

Beckson, Karl, and Ganz, Arthur. *A Reader's Guide to Literary Terms: A Dictionary.* New York: Farrar, Straus and Giroux.

Planned by the authors as "a guide . . . extensive enough for the teacher or writer yet clear enough for the student or the general reader." The entries have been chosen on the basis of their usefulness and include terms from poetry, criticism, fiction, and the drama, as well as discussions of movements in literary history. A subject index lists the terms most frequently encountered in a particular area. In the language of one critic, "this . . . reference book fills a long-standing need for concise definitions of all the terms of grammar, prosody, and versification, figurative, rhetorical, and solecistic language, from 'abecedarius' to 'zeugma' . . . a book that is not only useful but enjoyable to read . . ." Dr. Beckson has taught at Columbia, at Hunter College, etc. Dr. Ganz teaches at Rutgers University.

Benbow, John. *Manuscript and Proof: The Preparation of Manuscript for the Printer and the Handling of the Proofs.* New York: Oxford University Press.

What an author or reviewer needs to know about copy, editing, permissions, illustrations, order of pages, indexing, proofreading, etc.

Benét, William Rose, Editor. *The Reader's Encyclopedia.* New York: Thomas Y. Crowell Co.

Famous for its wide-ranging contents, this encyclopedia of world literature in a single volume concerns itself with every field of special interest to readers. Its thousands of entries include biographies of poets, playwrights, novelists, essayists and belles-lettrists from antiquity to the present, plot summaries, literary terms, sketches of principal characters, etc.

Berger, Edmund, M.D. *The Writer and Psychoanalysis.* New York: Doubleday & Co., Inc.

An exploration into those hidden drives and repressions which lead to productivity or creative sterility. Said to be the first time that the creative writing process has been viewed through the psychiatric-psychoanalytic microscope.

Brown, Curtis. *Contacts.* New York: Harper & Row.

Reminiscences of an internationally known literary agent on his "contacts [with] a great variety of interesting persons and personages—mostly writers."

Brown, Francis, Editor. *Opinions and Perspectives from the New York Times Book Review.* Boston: Houghton Mifflin Co.

This volume is described in the Introduction by Mr. Brown, editor of the *New York Times* Sunday Book Review, as "book talk, good book talk . . . the variety of literary experience and expression essential to an appreciation of what men and women during the past decade have been thinking and writing and, yes, reading." Authors of the sixty-two essays are the big names of contemporary literature—personages eminent and diverse. The pieces herein, chosen from a decade of *Times* Sunday book sections, are, in the language of Mr. Brown, "extremely selective . . . yet, paradoxically perhaps . . . representative . . . (possessing) long-time value and (making) as much of a contribution today as the day they first were printed." Another book by Mr. Brown which should interest reviewers is *Raymond of the Times* (Norton), about Henry J. Raymond who was also first editor of *Harper's* Magazine as well as the *Times*.

Burack, A. S., Editor. *The Writer's Handbook*. Boston: The Writer, Inc.

A volume which merits the brief but apt description of "a complete reference library for free-lance writers." Instruction in all major areas of writing, with advice from many successful and highly regarded practitioners. Information about markets, literary agents, and other relevant data.

Burke, W. J., and Howe, Will D. Augmented and revised by Irving Weiss. *American Authors and Books*. New York: Crown Publishers, Inc.

An encyclopedia of American books, authors, periodicals, organizations, and other pertinent data relating to the literary world. The 17,000 entries herein cover some 8,000 authors and editors, 600 novels, 700 magazines, 600 poems, 600 characters from novels and plays, 450 pen names, 200 short stories, 200 plays, 100 famous songs and hymns, and much more similar material, including anthologies, reference works, histories, etc.

Cairns, Huntington. *H. L. Mencken: The American Scene: A Reader*. New York: Alfred A. Knopf, Inc.

In appraisal of this most recent of the books dealing with

the work of the former editor of the *American Mercury,* Alfred A. Knopf, who was publisher of this magazine, has this to say: "Familiar with the entire body of Mencken's writings, Huntington Cairns has made a selection which presents not only old favorites but fresh material that even the most ardent Mencken aficionados may not have read before. He has also written remarkably fresh and perceptive commentary on his selections, and has prefaced the volume with one of the most interesting essays on Mencken that I have ever read . . . an excellent introduction for those younger readers to whom Mencken (is) only a name, and a splendid refresher for us older admirers of the work of one whose like we shall not see again."

————. *A Manual of Style, Containing Typographical Rules Governing the Publications of the University of Chicago Together with Specimens of Type Used at the University of Chicago Press.* Chicago: The University of Chicago Press.

This is probably the most widely used of the style books. It covers in great detail and with obvious authority a variety of technical topics, such as planning a book, capitalization, use of italics, quotations, spelling and abbreviations, punctuation, division of words, footnotes, bibliographies, legends and captions, tables, formulas, etc. But many writers prefer the U. S. Government Printing Office *Style Manual* and its Word Division supplement.

Davison, Dorothy, Editor. *Book Review Digest.* New York: H. W. Wilson Co.

This valuable cumulative reference, available at most libraries, includes quotes from reviews of fiction and non-fiction and enables one to learn what various reviewers have thought of a book.

Drury, Francis K. W., and Simnett, W. E. *What Books Shall I Read?* Boston: Houghton Mifflin Co.

A guide to the art of intelligent reading, including a survey of the outstanding books in each branch of literature.

Fernald, James C. *Funk & Wagnalls Standard Handbook of Synonyms, Antonyms & Prepositions*. New York: Funk & Wagnalls Co.

Soule, Richard. *A Dictionary of English Synonyms*. Boston: Little, Brown & Co.

————. *Webster's Dictionary of Synonyms*. Springfield, Mass.: G. & C. Merriam Co.

Of much potential value to the book reviewer is a book of synonyms and antonyms; these are three recommended volumes.

Fischer, John, and Silvers, Robert B., Editors. *Writing in America*. New Brunswick, N. J.: Rutgers University Press.

Most of the material contained in this volume previously appeared in a special supplement in *Harper's Magazine*; included here are such famous pieces as Elizabeth Hardwick's "The Decline of Book Reviewing" and Archibald MacLeish's "On the Teaching of Writing."

Freeman, William. *Dictionary of Fictional Characters*. Boston: The Writer, Inc.

Covering more than 2,000 classic, semi-classic, and modern works by 500 British and American authors, this valuable and useful reference work contains the names of over 20,000 fictitious characters from novels, short stories, poems, plays, and operas written in the English language during the past six centuries. The entries are listed alphabetically.

Grannis, Chandler B., Editor. *What Happens in Book Publishing*. New York: Columbia University Press.

Twenty-one leaders in the book publishing industry, each an authority in his or her field, are the authors of this survey of all aspects of writing, editing, printing, promotion, and sale of books. Each chapter ends with a list of books and articles which are recommended for further reading. The Foreword is by Frederic G. Melcher of *Publishers' Weekly*.

Gross, Gerald, Editor. *Publishers on Publishing*. New York: The Universal Library—Grosset & Dunlap.

This is said to be the first compendium of writings about publishing by the men who have known the business best—the publishers thmselves. Drawing upon the memoirs, recollections, articles, and talks of more than 30 of the leaders in this phase of the communications field, Mr. Gross has produced a volume of great interest and value to those who would know more about the book world, especially reviewers. Some of the big publishing names which add lustre to this volume are Walter Hines Page, Henry Holt, Bennett Cerf, Alfred A. Knopf, John Farrar, George Haven Putnam, and Frank Nelson Doubleday.

Haines, Helen E. *Living with Books: The Art of Book Selection*. New York: Columbia University Press.

Over and above its value to those associated with libraries, this volume, now in a second edition, is potentially useful to the reviewer and general reader. As Miss Haines says, "My aim has been to simplify and reduce technical and bibliographical detail and to stimulate . . . exploration and discovery . . . in certain great regional divisions of literature." The author, who has also written *Living with Books* and *What's in a Novel,* was honored by the establishment of a scholarship in her name at the School of Library Science, University of Southern California, where she performed valuable service for many years.

Hart, James D. *The Oxford Companion to American Literature.* New York: Oxford University Press.

A one-volume reference library for the general reader and the student of American literature. Within its pages is an amazing wealth of information, valuable to the reviewer, about American writers, books, periodicals, newspapers, and a diversity of related topics. This is really much more than a ready reference to the literature of a nation. It is, in the words of the compiler, an effort "to deal briefly with the American mind and the American scene as these are reflected in and influenced by American literature."

An idea of the scope of this work may be given by saying that it includes biographies and bibliographies of principal American authors, with information about their style and subject-matter; some nine hundred summaries and descriptions of important American novels, stories, essays, poems, and plays; definitions and historical outlines of literary schools and movements; and data on literary societies, magazines, anthologies, cooperative publications, literary awards, book collectors, and other matters relating to writing in America.

Jones, Llewellyn. *How to Criticize Books.* New York: W. W. Norton and Company.

A volume intended both for reviewers and "that constantly growing class of people who contribute in any way to the criticism, guidance, or even the description, of what is going on in the world of thought"—by a literary editor of the Chicago *Evening Post.*

Jovanovich, William. *Now, Barabbas.* New York: Harper & Row.

The man who became president of Harcourt, Brace and Company (now Harcourt, Brace & World, Inc.) when only thirty-four has been described by the London *Spectator* thus: "William Jovanovich is a special sort of publisher . . . who, in the words of a disinterested fellow-publisher, 'not only publishes good books—he could write them.' " *Now, Barabbas* proves the point. It is a volume highly to be recommended for reviewers. It reflects the personality and philosophy of one who believes that "publishing is . . . a primarily civilizing enterprise and like orderly government . . . is central to a humanistic society."

Kunitz, Stanley J. and Haycraft, Howard, Editors. *Twentieth Century Authors.* New York: The H. W. Wilson Co.

A biographical dictionary of modern literature, with almost 2,000 biographies of writers of this century, plus many pictures, lists of principal works, etc.

————. *Literary Market Place, The Business Directory of American Book Publishing.* New York: R. R. Bowker Co.

An annual directory giving the information most desired by those active in the world of books: an alphabetical list of the most active book publishers in the United States (including names of chief personnel and number and type of books published), names of newspapers and magazines printing book reviews, information on various editorial and manufacturing services, etc.

Magill, Frank N., Editor. *Cyclopedia of Literary Characters*. New York: Harper & Row.

Individual identification and description of each of more than 16,000 characters from some 1,300 novels, dramas, and epics, drawn from world literature. Characters in each book appear together, in the order of diminishing importance. Book titles are arranged alphabetically in the text, and a special character index, also arranged alphabetically, follows the text. Next is an author index of all those whose works are represented in this book, which also appears under the title of *Masterplots Cyclopedia of Literary Characters*.

Miers, Earl Schenck, and Ellis, Richard, Editors. *Bookmaking and Kindred Amenities*. New Brunswick: Rutgers University Press, in association with The Hadden Craftsmen.

A collection of essays by Beatrice Ward, Richard Ellis, Carl Purington Rollins, Bennett A. Cerf, George Stevens, Philip Van Doren Stern, Earl Schenck Miers, Lewis Gannett, Lawrence Thompson, Lawrence Gomme, and Arthur W. Rushmore, with an introduction by the editors.

Mott, Frank Luther. *Rewards of Reading*. New York: Henry Holt and Co.

A popular treatise on literary appreciation which stresses two themes: "first, reading must be *enjoyed* if it is to be worth much; and, second, all good reading is very personal —it is *personal* as regards both the author who puts himself into the writing of it and the reader who puts himself into its perusal." The author won a Pulitzer Prize—winner in history with his *A History of American Magazines*.

Mulgan, John E. *The Concise Oxford Dictionary of English Literature*. New York: Oxford University Press.

This is based on Sir Paul Harvey's *Oxford Companion to English Literature*. All entries which deal with major matters of English literature are essentially the same as those in Sir Paul's book, except that many of them have been reduced in length. The volume is a veritable encyclopedia of authors and works of importance, characters from books and plays, and mythological and historical entries which relate directly to English literature. Articles which summarize periods of literary history and general literary subjects in concise form are a feature of this book.

Newquist, Roy. *Counterpoint*. New York: Rand McNally & Co.

This book attempts to answer such questions as these: How seriously do writers take themselves, their work, and the world about them? What are their working methods, their attitudes toward research, their advice to young would-be writers? What kind of people are writers? How qualified are published authors for the roles they consciously or unconsciously assume in the entertainment, opinion-shaping, and education of millions of readers. To provide the answers Mr. Newquist, himself a successful book reviewer, herein brings together 63 interviews with authors, columnists, and publishers—all of such eminence as to command great attention and much interest. The Foreword is by Mark Van Doren who is highly complimentary of Mr. Newquist's skill as an interviewer. He is, says this eminent author and former Columbia University teacher, "one of the rare souls in whose presence we prattle—without, however, ceasing to be serious. Indeed, it is in the endeavor to be serious with him, and so to tell him all we think we understand, that we find ourselves going on and on into disclosures we never made before."

Nicholson, Margaret. *A Manual of Copyright Practice for Writers, Publishers, and Agents*. New York: Oxford University Press.

A clearly written, well-organized and practical book on copyright procedure and practice.

Perry, Bliss. *A Study of Prose Fiction*. Boston: Houghton Mifflin Co.

An outline for the study of the art of prose fiction. First published in 1902, it has since, in the language of the autor, "been reprinted so often that I have no excuse for any errors of fact which it may still contain." This book was quite helpful in the preparation of the chapter on fiction in this handbook, and can be studied with profit by those who anticipate doing much fiction reviewing.

Prakken, Sarah, Editor. *Books in Print*. New York: R. R. Bowker Co.

An author-title-series index to *The Publishers' Trade List Annual.*

Prescott, Orville. *Five-Dollar Gold Piece: The Development of a Point of View*. New York: Random House.

The autobiography of a distinguished critic, whose daily book reviews have appeared in the New York *Times* for more than twenty years.

———. *The Publishers' Trade List Annual.* New York: R. R. Bowker Company.

A compilation of all of the catalogues of American publishers.

Reynolds, Paul R. *The Writing and Selling of Fiction.* New York: Doubleday & Co.

The most recent book by a distinguished New York literary agent who has also written *The Writing and Selling of Non-Fiction, The Writer and His Markets,* and *The Writing Trade.*

Richards, I. A. *How to Read a Page: A Course in Efficient Reading.* Boston: Beacon Press.

A guide to improvement in reading through a study of the main meanings of key words, by the co-author of *The Meaning of Meaning,* at present director of the Commission on English Language Studies at Harvard University.

Roget, Peter Mark. *Thesaurus of English Words and Phrases.* New York: Grosset & Dunlap.

This is the authorized American edition of Roget's *Thesaurus*; there are several different editions, one done in "dictionary form," etc.

Steiner-Prag, Mrs. Eleanor, Editor. *American Book Trade Directory.* New York: R. R. Bowker Co.

Published since 1915 this work features an up-to-date list

of book sellers, publishers, wholesalers, book trade associations, periodicals, reference tools, and other pertinent information about the American book market. The lists are alphabetical by states and cities for the U.S.A. and Canada.

Stevens, George. *Lincoln's Doctor's Dog and Other Famous Best Sellers*. Philadelphia: J. B. Lippincott Company.

A commentary—factual, thoughtful, and delightfully written—on how books come to be best sellers. Its author was editor of *The Saturday Review of Literature* at the time the book was published. The title of the volume is based on the fact that books about Lincoln, about doctors, and about dogs usually sell well. A best seller, therefore, should be a book about Lincoln's doctor's dog.

Svatik, Olga, Editor. *Literary and Library Prizes*. New York: R. R. Bowker Co.

Revised and enlarged periodically to keep it up-to-date, this volume describes the major American, British, Canadian, French and German prizes—as well as the Nobel Prize for Literature—and lists their winners over the years.

Thompson, Nina R., Editor. *Cumulative Book Index*. New York: H. W. Wilson Co.

Begun in 1898, the *Cumulative Book Index* since 1928 has been an author, title, and subject index to current books in the English language published in all countries. Government publications, pamphlets, and ephemera are excluded. Books are entered by author, subject, and editor. There are also numerous title, series, translator, and illustrator listings. All entries are in a single alphabetical list. Price, publisher, binding, paging, edition, date of publication, and

Library of Congress card order number are given for each book. A directory of publishers is appended.

Turner, Mary C. *The Bookman's Glossary.* New York: R. R. Bowker Co.

Designed to be a practical guide for those interested in the terminology used in the production and distribution of books new and old—not necessarily the technical language of the print shop or the paper trade, but the words in common usage in a bookstore, publisher's office, library, or among book collectors.

Warburg, Fredric. *An Occupation for Gentlemen.* Boston: Houghton Mifflin Co.

This behind-the-scenes account of the life of a book publisher grew out of the following question asked the author at a party given by his firm to launch the new novel of a promising young author: "Tell me . . . is publishing an occupation for gentlemen or is it a real business?" To read this book is to conclude that the answer is yes for both parts of the question. Publishing is an occupation for gentlemen and is also a real business. As Thomas Mann says in a passage which Mr. Warburg quotes, "What a glorious occupation, this mixture of business sense and strategic friendship with the spirit! What a noble way to gain a livelihood!" Or as Mr. Warburg himself puts it, "Publishing deals with the highest achievements of man's creativity. And the publisher himself is a creator of an unusual and special type."

Warren, Dale. *What Is a Book? Thoughts about Writing.* Boston: Houghton Mifflin Co.

"What is a book? 'A book's a book,' retorted Mary Lamb,

and that was the end of it. One editor at least is inclined to disagree, and those whose convictions are recorded in (these) pages likewise appear to believe that the question cannot be answered so simply." So writes Mr. Warren, who at the time was publicity director of Houghton Mifflin Company.

Contributors to his valuable anthology are Ellen Glasgow, Rafael Sabatini (historical fiction), Gertrude Atherton, Jeanette Eaton, Phyllis Bottome, Edward J. O'Brien (short story), Frances Frost, Archibald MacLeish, Esther Forbes, James Norman Hall, John Livingston Lowes, etc.

Weber, H. Sherwood, Editor. *Good Reading*. New York: The New American Library of World Literature, Inc.

Prepared by the Committee on College Reading, this guide to the world's best books contains concise descriptions of over five hundred books from all periods and fields, plus a comprehensive listing of the best paperbound books.

Weeks, Edward. *Breaking into Print: An Editor's Advice on Writing*. Boston: The Writer, Inc.

*Breaking into Print* will be of much value to those interested in writing, be they producers, potential producers, or consumers. Topics included are incentives to and rewards of authorship; methods of various writers; marketing manuscripts; trends in literary forms, with special reference to the place of the essay, short story, and poetry in contemporary letters; censorship; arguments for and against literary prizes; and popular tastes in books.

"Rereading my youthful pronouncements [in *This Trade of Writing*] I realized how greatly the publishing world has changed since I wrote that book," comments Mr. Weeks.

"The enormous revival in reading which began with the return to the campus of the G.I.'s in 1946 and has been further amplified by their children who are now in college; the rising and intensified interest in non-fiction, in works of history, foreign affairs and social science; the blizzard of paperbacks . . . and the high costs of the hard-cover book which have narrowed the opportunity for the new author, changes like these have compelled me to write about a very different set of circumstances from those I perceived when I entered the literary field in 1923, and what began as a revision came to be a fresh book . . ."

For some years editor of the *Atlantic Monthly* and writer of "The Peripatetic Reviewer," Mr. Weeks was chairman of the Massachusetts committee which, after a three-year fight, reformed the book censorship laws of the Commonwealth.

Winans, Leonard G. *The Book: From Manuscript to Market.* New York: Grosset and Dunlap.

The story of how the intangible becomes the tangible in the realm of ideas. Subjects treated include ancient origins of the modern book, the place of the author and the publisher and the relationship between the two, the various ways in which manuscripts are translated into the printed page, engravings, press work, and binding and design.

In connection with the last point, he says—and the reviewer should have a special interest in this—that "a great deal of credit should go to Alfred Knopf for bringing . . . a feeling for design in the ordinary book of fiction. It was a long time before other American publishers caught on to the fact that Borzoi (the Knopf trademark) books were attracting readers for reasons other than the text matter contained in the books alone. Knopf books stressed the value of design—in stamping, two-colored title pages, and the cloth used in binding. He made people type conscious and paper conscious by telling them the names of the types used and the quality of the paper upon which they were printed. American book publishers and American book readers owe Mr. Knopf a debt of gratitude for making books things of beauty as well as a joy forever. . . ."

Wittenberg, Philip. *The Law of Literary Property.* Cleveland and New York: The World Publishing Co.

An authority on the legal aspects of letters for more than forty years, Mr. Wittenberg has lectured on the law of literary property at Columbia University and the New School of Social Research. This book covers such topics as infringement, fair use, quotation, burlesque, permissions, international copyright, the nature of literary property; history of statutory copyrights; plagiarism, piracy, and mind-picking; theft of names and titles; remedies for piracy and infringement; literature and indecency; libel; agents; contracts; and various rights, including motion picture and radio.

* * *

Those who review books should, of course, be familiar with libraries, their holdings and procedures, and the better reference works, especially those which relate to or are potentially helpful in reviewing the book under consideration.

The first requisite to effective use of a library is a reasonable understanding of the card catalog, in which there are three kinds of cards. These are referred to as author cards, title cards, and subject cards.

The author card has the author's name on the first line, written always with the surname first.

The title card has the title of the book on the first line. There is a title card for each book in the library.

The subject card has the subject with which the book deals on the first line.

A typical author card will give the following information: the call number of the book; the author's complete name (this may be followed by the years of his birth and death); the title of the book, and subtitle if there is one; the name of the publisher; and the copyright date.

The title card and subject card gives basically the same information.

Abbreviations and terms frequently used on catalog cards are:

Bibliography—a list of books on a given subject.

Books of reference—additional reference books on a topic.

cm.—centimeters, show the size of the book.

comp.—compiler.

Contains bibliographies—list of books on a given subject.

diagrs.—diagrams.

ed.—edition, editor, edited.

enl. or enlar.—enlarged, that is, more material has been added.

fold—folded, as a folded map, etc.

front.—frontispiece, that is, the illustration which faces the title page.

In portfolio—in a case or an envelope which contains maps, plans, etc.

incl.—including.

illus.—illustrator, illustrated, illustration, or illustrations.

mounted pl.—mounted, full page illustrations.

pseud.—pseudonym or pen name.

References at end of each chapter—there is a bibliography at the end of each chapter.

rev.—revised, that is, the material has been changed and brought up to date.

tr.—translator or translated by.

*Arrangement of Books in a Library.*—No matter how small the particular library, the books are arranged according to a definite plan. The most common plan in use in public libraries and schools in the United States is the Dewey Decimal System of Classification. Melvin Dewey in 1876 set up this plan which includes ten major classes with as many subclasses as may be necessary.

The ten classes of books in the Dewey system are:

Class 000-099 General Works.
Class 100-199 Philosophy.
Class 200-299 Religion.
Class 300-399 Social Sciences.
Class 400-499 Philology.
Class 500-599 Pure Science.
Class 600-699 Useful Arts and Applied Science.
Class 700-799 Fine Arts, Recreation.
Class 800-899 Literature, Belles-Lettres.
Class 900-999 History, Geography and Travel, Biography.

In order to understand the arrangement of books in a library it is necessary not only to understand the large general classes but also to understand how a given class is subdivided. Following is an example of how the 500 class is subdivided, according to the Dewey Decimal System. The 500 class deals with science. It is divided into ten subdivisions, as is each of the ten main classes.

500-509 Pure Science.
510-519 Mathematics.
520-529 Astronomy.
530-539 Physics.
540-549 Chemistry.
550-559 Geology.
560-569 Paleontology.
570-579 Biology.
580-589 Botany.
590-599 Zoology.

Each of these subdivisions is divided in turn into ten parts. For example, the 510-519 class, which deals with Mathematics is subdivided as follows:

510 Mathematics.
511 Arithmetic.
512 Algebra.
513 Geometry.
514 Trigonometry.
515 Descriptive Geometry.
516 Analytic Geometry, Quaternions.
517 Calculus.
518 (unassigned).
519 Probabilities.

Each of these subdivisions is again subdivided and the subdivision is indicated by the use of the decimal. For example, the 511 class—Arithmetic—is divided:

511. Arithmetic.
511.1 Systems of Arithmetic.

511.2 Notation and numeration; fundamental rules; abacus.
511.3 Prime numbers.
511.4 Fractions.
511.5 Analysis; permutation and combination.
511.6 Proportion and progression.
511.7 Involution and evolution.
511.8 Mercantile rules; interest; alligation; mensuration; gaging.
511.9 Problems and tables.

# XV

# THE BOOK PAGE

*A book may be amusing with numerous errors, or it may be very dull without a single absurdity.*

—Oliver Goldsmith.

*Learn to write well, or not to write at all.*

—John Dryden.

*Books that you may carry to the fire and hold readily in your hand, are the most useful after all.*

—Samuel Johnson.

## THE BOOK PAGE

THE BOOK PAGE or section should, within the limits of its size and periodicity, cover the news and opinion of the book world with the same adequacy and proportion that the remainder of the paper reports the general news. It should be for its realm what the sports pages are for the various phases of athletics, amateur and professional, or what the financial pages are for business and Wall Street.

Like the newspaper as a whole, the book page or section should contain:

1. *News items*—stories of one or more paragraphs reporting objectively current developments in the book world.

2. *Human-interest stories*—little items which make primarily an emotional appeal. Incidents that are amusing, sad, tragic, etc., fall in this category.

3. *Feature articles*—the longer, more important reviews are, as was brought out in earlier chapter, actually feature articles, i.e., they are informative, entertaining, worthwhile pieces of writing, interesting in themselves, aside from whether or not one has read or plans to read the books about which they are written.

4. *Editorials*—many editors of book pages, just as do sports editors, have a column of their own. Herein they comment, subjectively, on a diversity of literary topics. This is really the editorial of the page or the section. It is essentially interpretative or explanatory, and reflects the policy of the page and its editor, just as the editorial page is the

mouthpiece of the editor, publisher, and owners of the paper as a whole.

5. *Poetry*—Poems serve both an aesthetic and utilitarian purpose on the book page. They add that grace and charm, that literary flavor which is peculiar to the verse form. And they aid in makeup in various ways: they fill gaps here and there on the page; they may easily be boxed or indented; and they provide that contrast and variety so essential to good typography.

6. *Illustrations*—This is very definitely an era of pictorial journalism. The popularity of such magazines as *Life* and *Look* are eloquent testimony to this. The book page, like the rest of the paper, should carry as many good and appropriate illustrations as the budget will allow. Photographs of authors are, of course, a stand-by for the literary section. But there are many other possibilities—reproductions of the art work on jackets; photographs and reproductions of portraits of subjects of biographies (particularly if these be hitherto unpublished or not known to have existed); sketches and other original works of art; some local worthy in the act of reading or purchasing a new book or current best seller in his field (for example, your congressman thumbing through Dean Acheson's *Morning and Noon,* or the local little theatre director reading Helen Hayes' *A Gift of Joy*); or an author in the act of autographing his new book at the local bookstore. Although still pictures will always have their place on the book page, action shots will do much to enliven the appearance and appeal of the section.

7. *Advertisement*—Advertising on a book page is tangible evidence that hard-headed businessmen feel that the page is being read by a sufficient number of literary-minded and

solvent individuals to make it a good place to stimulate sales for their products. Actually, every book page should carry enough advertising to pay its cost of production with a reasonable margin of profit. Among those who should advertise in this section and whose business should be regularly solicited are book publishers; local bookstores; book departments of department stores; stationery and office supply firms; drugstores having book and magazine counters; lending libraries; those responsible for local lectures by authors and other public figures; those sponsoring concerts, art exhibits, and other gatherings to which an admission fee is charged; national book clubs; and all those whose business in any way impinges on books, their authors, and their readers.

8. *Regular departments*—such items as a daily or weekly list of the new books, with the name of the author, the publisher, the price, and possibly a one-sentence description (one newspaper calls this "Latest Books from the Press"; another simply "Published Today"); current best sellers, with the emphasis on local tastes (The Atlanta *Constitution* has carried this feature under the heading "What Atlanta Is Reading Now"); a survey of new offerings in the ever-popular detective-mystery story classifications; occasional summaries of trends and new titles among books for children; seasonal articles, such as appropriate gift books near Christmas (often such articles can be tied in with accompanying seasonal advertising); a regular question-and-answer feature about books ("The Reader's Clinic" is the title one paper gave to such a column, wherein a member of the local library staff answered all kinds of questions and directed readers to good books in various fields); literary let-

ters from foreign countries (this feature is probably restricted to larger papers, such as the New York *Times* with its regular letters from London and other foreign capitals—though occasionally such letters should not be out of the realm of possibility for almost any publication); syndicated articles; and letters from readers.

This last point merits special comment. A letter department, as old Ben Franklin so well knew when he used to write as well as answer "letters to the editor," is an almost certain way to stimulate interest among readers and to enlarge circulation. Note the good use which *Time* and *Life* magazines and the New York *Times*—to mention but three examples—have made of their letter section. *Time* at one period was getting so many good letters that it was able to publish a special supplement composed wholly of letters and its own editorial repartee.

There are a few simple rules regarding letters which the book editor should bear in mind: (a) all communications should be signed; (b) there should be a fixed maximum number of words (The Atlanta *Journal* once headed its letter-column with this Shakespearean admonition: "Go, write it in a martial-hand, be brief—it is no matter how witty"); (c) the content of the letter should conform to the dictates of good taste and the laws of libel.

9. *Cartoons and comics*—Although one does not ordinarily associate cartoons and comics with book pages, actually a number of the so-called panel cartoons would be as appropriate on the literary page as the editorial page. Some excellent cartoons that have a connection with books appear in the *Saturday Review* and *The New Yorker*.

*Reviews*—A good part of the book page or section will, of

course, consist of reviews. Reviews, however, as was stated in an earlier chapter, are a combination of the news story, editorial, and feature article—all of which have already been commented upon.

The book editor is concerned not only with what appears on his page, but the *sources* of such material.

The reviews of new books ordinarily are written by:

1. *Staff writers*—reporters, editorial writers, and others who like to read and who are glad to have access to the new books and the extra compensation which sometimes goes with reviewing.

2. *Regular contributors*—college professors, doctors, lawyers, ministers, members of the local library staff, and other specialists who also like to keep in touch with current thought, especially in the fields of their special interests, and who have a flair for writing.

3. *Press services and syndicates*—The Associated Press, United Press International, and many of the syndicates provide reviews of individual new books as well as surveys and special columns devoted to books. The book editor can arrange with the managing editor, the head of the copy desk, or whichever editor opens the syndicated matter to put aside all items bearing on books and authors for his department.

4. *Occasional contributors*—As contrasted with the regular contributors are those occasional reviewers who generally write about a book in response to a special request or assignment by the editor. To illustrate, *The Hustler's Handbook* by Bill Veeck and Ed Linn appears, and the book editor in Nashville or St. Louis asks the head coach of a nearby college baseball team to do the review. This will probably be the first and last such literary undertaking of the coach (ac-

tually the review may be "ghosted," i.e., written by another), but this in no way detracts from its interest or value.

Facts for news items, human interest stories, and feature articles for the book page come from the publicity releases of the various publishing houses, interviews with authors, book dealers, lending libraries, press services, and syndicates.

Poetry may be secured from local writers or may be reproduced, with proper permission, from other newspapers, magazines, or books.

Illustrations are available from among the photographs and mats supplied by publishers, from similar material originating with press services and syndicates, and from the work of local or staff photographers.

Not only what is to appear on the book page and how this is to be secured, but the arrangement of the content, the *makeup* of the page, is a problem and responsibility of the book editor.

There are essentially two plans of makeup for the book page:

1. To vary the page day by day or week by week, featuring first this and then that, very much in the manner of some front pages. This means that one week there will be many pictures, large pictures, large headlines. Another week, the pictures may be smaller and fewer and the display more restrained. Just as the quality of the news (the number of persons interested in an item and the extent to which they are interested) determines relative news values and how front pages are made up, so the news of the book page may determine its appearance. This plan makes, of course, for variety, and a great many editors think variety attracts readers and increases circulation.

2. To have a basic pattern for the page, very much as most newspapers have a standard makeup for the editorial page. Certain regular features appear in their accustomed places with what the printer calls "standing heads." There is a regular schedule for captions or headlines. A particular face of type, distinctive to the page, but harmonizing with the remainder of the paper, is used. Such a page is not, however, wholly without variety. Picture sizes and positions will, of course, differ from issue to issue, and there will be other minor departures from a monotonous uniformity. The basic pattern should, however, be apparent at all times.

Sports pages and dramatic sections often reflect the personalities of their conductors. Their pages become the lengthened shadows of those who are responsible for them. The same thing is true, and should be true, of many book pages. Mention the *Saturday Review* and one thinks of the thoughtful honest comments of Granville Hicks. Recall "The Library" during the heyday of *The American Mercury* and one is reminded of H. L. Mencken's amusing, irreverent, penetrating reviews, many of which were of what Harry Hansen calls the "springboard" variety; i.e., the book served as a point of departure for an illuminating and witty essay —sometimes sardonic—on what the author knew about the subject and possibly other related and unrelated topics.

Sinclair Lewis once wrote of William Lyon Phelps, "He remains the one man in his generation of college teachers who has been most able to inoculate students, even quite stupid ones, apparently formed only for the purpose of falling with virile grunts upon pigskin ovoids, with his own passion for the secret joys of good literature."

There is a lesson for book editors and reviewers generally

in the last part of this quotation—a "passion for the secret joys of good literature." That, in essence, should be the goal in all reviewing—to impart to others one's own enthusiasm for the good, the beautiful, the practically useful, and the worthwhile in current books.

# XVI

# HOW THE EXPERTS DO IT

*Some books are to be tasted, others to be swallowed, and some few to be chewed and digested.*

*Reading maketh a full man, conference a ready man, and writing an exact man.*

*In books we converse with the wise, as in action with fools.*

—Francis Bacon.

## HOW THE EXPERTS DO IT

IN ANOTHER CHAPTER, various distinguished book reviewers were quoted on the hows, whys, and wherefores of their art. They discoursed sagely on what should and should not be done. In this section, specimens of reviews by these and other well-known names in the literary world are offered.

Most of the illustrations herein assembled bear out the instructions, advice, and suggestions of foregoing pages. All rules, of course, have their exceptions, or in the language of the popular saying, "the exception proves the rule." Also, it should be borne in mind that as a reviewer becomes a personage, or to put it another way, as a reviewer becomes a critic, his work naturally leans more in the direction of the subjective. This point is made because it is almost inevitable that "big name" reviewers have increasing difficulty—and justifiably so, perhaps—in being as objective in their treatment of a work of literature as a less well-known reviewer.

In some instances, the reviews included have been chosen by the reviewer himself; in others, by the writer of this book. In both cases, an effort has been made to select reviews which are (1) illustrative of the style and manner of the reviewer; and (2) which deal with books of more than ephemeral interest.

### VAN ALLEN BRADLEY

Literary editor of the Chicago *Daily News* since 1948, Mr. Bradley has also been an editorial writer for this newspaper and is author of the syndicated rare book column, "Gold in Your Attic." He has been a lecturer and teacher at the Medill School of Journalism, Northwestern University; and an officer of many educational and professional groups. Mr. Bradley's books include *Music for the Millions, Gold in Your Attic,* and *How to Predict What People Will Buy.*

THE LIFE OF DYLAN THOMAS. By Constantine FitzGibbon. Atlantic-Little, Brown, $7.95.

A friend of ours who is internationally known as an authority on the difficult poetry of the late Dylan Thomas remarked the other evening that because he knew little about the writer's life he had turned down an invitation to review Constantine FitzGibbon's biography.

The fact is, as we told him, that perhaps the most rewarding aspect of this carefully researched (and authorized) life of the Welsh poet is Mr. FitzGibbon's constant effort to sort out and make clear for us those environmental influences that shaped both the complex, soaring patterns of his verse and his tragic destiny.

It is a brilliantly successful book, a creative triumph of the biographer's art. It treats its subject with respect for the unquestioned fire of genius that flamed within him. It is filled with personal affection that never for a moment excuses or condones those negative aspects of the poet's life that made of it the dark drama we know, but rather seeks to understand. It's a painful, beautiful book.

Through anecdote after anecdote, many of them personally observed or obtained, we begin to make sense of this extraordinary man who breathed new life into English poetry in his time with the greatest lyric talent since Yeats, who recited his verses and the lines of other men with the voice of an angel, who endeared himself to audiences of true poetry lovers as well as mere celebrity seekers on four trips to America, who looked worse in his rumpled clothes than any public figure since Heywood Broun, who stole, and cheated, and sponged, and lied, who brawled and drank himself to death at 39. Nothing is hidden here; everything is laid bare.

Mr. FitzGibbon's serious purpose—to portray the true man as distinct from the legendary figure—is apparent from the opening chapter. He spends a great deal of time in carefully showing us how the very remoteness of Thomas' childhood home of Swansea, in Wales, gave his developing originality as an artist the protection it needed and could never have had had he been exposed in his youth to the copycat literary life of a larger center such as London. He shows us also how the home life of the Thomases nurtured his talents and spurred his imagination: His father, who taught English in the Swansea grammar school, insisted on reading Shakespeare to Dylan when he was only 4. The effect, says Mr. FitzGibbon, was profound and lasting. A sickly child, he was coddled by his mother, was often lonely, started writing poems at about 8 or 9 and boasted to his mother that he would some day be "better than Keats."

His decision to follow the life of a poet was clear-cut when at 16 he left the Swansea grammar school and, against his father's wish, declined a formal education. In the next three years he produced all the poems that would appear in his famous first book, "18 Poems," and most of those in his second, "25 Poems." He went on to London to live in 1934, began to gain a reputation with his poems and stories, met and unsuccessfully proposed to the novelist Pamela Hansford Johnson, who tried, unsuccessfully, to curb his beer-drinking habits, and finally, in 1946, met Caitlin Macnamara, the Irish writer who became the great love of his life.

The account of the married life of the Thomases has already been told by Caitlin Thomas in her memorable book, "Leftover Life to Kill," and it is retold here with sympathy and great understanding by Mr. FitzGibbon, who gives full credit at every turn to Caitlin, the loving mother of his children and "a good wife" to a genius in whom she believed desperately but one who never outgrew the attitudes and habits of a child.

This is not to say that Thomas was not utterly devoted to Caitlin. As Mr. FitzGibbon makes amply clear, his reputation as a woman chaser, while somewhat magnified by Thomas himself, was rather well earned, but every woman to whom he made love was in reality just Caitlin.

In the most moving passage in this book, he discusses the celebrated marital brawls of the Thomases, well publicized on Dylan's trips to America, and agrees with the novelist Ruthven Todd that it was "the public Dylan" (or what Todd calls "the instant Dylan") who was the cause of all their great unhappiness. It was, says Mr. FitzGibbon, "the life-and-soul of the saloon bar, the man who had to establish an apparently intimate relationship" with every man—"and, more dangerously and hatefully for Caitlin, with every woman"—who "became for her a contemptible and corrupt public figure."

"This was not what she had loved and married," says Thomas' biographer, "this amateur actor who was prepared to play the buffoon if that were the only way to attract attention, surrounded by yearning, admiring women and men, their faces creased by guffaws, whom she knew he despised but whose admiration and laughter he wanted and, increasingly, needed. Nor was this even the man she knew at home, the honest poet who took such pains that he would write and rewrite a line fifty or a hundred times until he was quite sure that he had achieved poetic truth."

Jealousy tore at Caitlin as the news of Dylan's infidelities came to her each time he went away from the home at Laugharne without her.

"It was to get steadily worse as he grew more famous, until at last it almost killed her love for him. With what pitiful weapons she could muster, and those encumbered by nappies and stewpots and dishcloths, she was fighting Dylan the entertainer, the character she hated, and who became increasingly Dylan the drunken buffoon, for the sake of Dylan the poet, whom she loved. It was worst of all, she thought, in America. And when she arrived in New York, where he was dying, and asked: 'Is the bloody man dead yet?' it was to the buffoon she referred, for the death of the poet broke her heart."

### David Dempsey

Mr. Dempsey is a free-lance writer who often comments on publishing trends and contemporary reader response. In the following review, which appeared in the New York *Times,* he writes about some of the books relating to John F. Kennedy which were published after the assassination of the President. This article* is an excellent example of how more than one book relating to the same theme may be included in a single review or article.

AMERICA THE BEAUTIFUL. In the Words of John F. Kennedy. By the editors of Country Beautiful Foundation, Elm Grove, Wis. Illustrated. Distributed by Doubleday & Co., New York.

THE BURDEN AND THE GLORY. Edited by Allan Nevins. New York and Evanston: Harper & Row.

A DAY IN THE LIFE OF PRESIDENT KENNEDY. By Jim Bishop. New York: Random House.

FOUR DAYS. Compiled by United Press International and American Heritage Magazine. Illustrated. New York: American Heritage Publishing Company.

JFK: Boyhood to White House. By Bruce Lee. Illustrated. Greenwich, Conn.: Fawcett Publications.

JOHN F. KENNEDY, PRESIDENT. By Hugh Sidey. Illustrated. New York: Atheneum.

THE JOHN F. KENNEDYS. By Mark Shaw. Illustrated. New York: Farrar, Straus & Co.

THE KENNEDY WIT. Edited by Bill Adler. Illustrated. New York: Citadel Press.

THE KENNEDY YEARS AND THE NEGRO. Edited by Doris E. Saunders. Illustrated. Chicago: Johnson Publishing Company.
THE MAGNIFICENT KENNEDY WOMEN. By Stanley P. Friedman. Illustrated. Danbury, Conn.: Monarch Books.
MR. KENNEDY AND THE NEGROES. By Harry Golden. Cleveland and New York: The World Publishing Company.
NOVEMBER TWENTY SIX NINETEEN HUNDRED SIXTY THREE. By Wendell Berry. Illustrated by Ben Shahn. Unpaged. New York: George Braziller.
ONCE THERE WAS A PRESIDENT. By S. J. Frolick. Illustrated. Unpaged. New York: Kanrom.
PORTRAIT OF A PRESIDENT. By William Manchester. New York: Macfadden-Bartell.
PROFILES IN COURAGE. By John F. Kennedy. New York and Evanston: Harper & Row.
THE SHINING MOMENTS: The Words and Moods of John F. Kennedy. Edited by Gerald Gardner. Illustrated. Unpaged. New York: Pocket Books.
SIX WHITE HORSES. By Candy Geer. Illustrated. Unpaged. Ann Arbor, Mich.: M. & W. Quill Publishing Company.
THAT SPECIAL GRACE. By Benjamin Bradlee. Illustrated. Unpaged. Philadelphia and New York: J. B. Lippincott Company.
THE TORCH IS PASSED. Compiled by The Associated Press. Illustrated. Distributed by The Daily News, New York.
A TRIBUTE TO JOHN F. KENNEDY. Edited by Pierre Salinger and Sander Vanocur. Illustrated. Chicago: Encyclopaedia Britannica. Distributed by Atheneum, New York.

If books and their readers are proof, John F. Kennedy commands an allegiance unmatched during his lifetime. Publishers, filling an emptiness in the American heart, continue to reaffirm the esteem and love which the late President's death evoked among the peoples of the world.

We are told that The Associated Press's memorial volume, *The Torch Is Passed,* has sold more than four million copies. United Press International-American Heritage's *Four Days,* now heading the best-seller list, claims an even larger sale. Bookstores stock an increasing range of titles—there are at least 20, including the paperbacks—and find there is no diminution of interest. People are buying these books who never bought a book before.

One may buy the Kennedy he wants. A collection of editorial tributes, edited by Pierre Salinger and Sander Vanocur, sees the man as we want to see him, not plain, but elegantly prepared for immortality, because frankly, we are a little apprehensive about historians, suspecting that Kennedy is safer in our hands than theirs.

Memorial albums of the assassination and its aftermath resemble those souvenir play programs which we save to prove to ourselves that what we saw was real. This is the martyred Kennedy. The mortal man is found in the "family" books, the quickie biographies and the picture albums, one of which is sent into the competition without a single word of text. But was any President or his family more photogenic; or for that matter, more photographed?

An obituary from *Newsweek* is deployed on the pages to resemble verse (it isn't). Wendell Berry has written a real poem, illustrated by Ben Shahn with his own grief but not his own best talent, for somehow the poetry and the drawings are overpowered by the event that inspired them. Harry Golden is more successful with a book that owes its inspiration to Kennedy, whom he calls "the second Great Emancipator," but the real value of which comes from Golden's own keen observation of race relations in the South.

The inspirational Kennedy speaks in *America the Beautiful,* a handsome assemblage of photographs for which the late President's words, taken from "previously unpublished writings," become extended captions to his own dream of America. *The Burden and the Glory* is a collection of addresses and Presidential papers written during his second and third years in office—the public Kennedy, and the man with which posterity will have to deal when the Kennedy known only to his intimates is lost. Finally, there is *Profiles in Courage,* reissued in a memorial edition—the Kennedy who takes his place alongside Woodrow Wilson and Theodore Roosevelt as someone who could turn his knowledge of history into a certain literary elegance.

When all this is said, there is something missing. In his short career, the President left behind him a good many unreplaced divots which most of his biographers have chosen to overlook. The driving, at times ruthlessly ambitious, Kennedy is not here. He emerges from these accounts free of the party politics that gave him power. But most of all, history itself is not here—the sense of inevitability that catapulted Lincoln into martyrdom and Franklin Roosevelt into greatness.

The issue of Union, from which Lincoln took his mandate, will never be separated from its most eloquent spokesman, nor will the Great Depression and World War II be remembered without F.D.R. By comparison, Kennedy lacked a clearcut and dramatic confrontation with a turning point in history. He came into office at a time when the nation found itself drifting aimlessly between prosperity and stagnation at home, and between war and peace abroad. The country needed to be awakened, to be convinced that issues existed. It was the President's mission to define these issues, and then move men to action.

The books capture some of this intention. On the Negro question, indeed, Mr. Golden's book captures all of it; and the Salinger-Vanocur anthology is filled with the President's wide-ranging idealism. But mostly these volumes recover the memories of a man. They are inspired by his charm, his youth, his war heroism, his fortune—Kennedy used to remark at political rallies, when he was running for the Senate, "I am the candidate who did not come up the hard way."

The Kennedys, in this respect, provided writers with an ideal substitute for a Royal Family. The yachting holidays off Newport, the state dinners and concerts, Jacqueline's painting—everything is here to assure us that a President can reign as well as govern. If he did not live to see the world "made safe for diversity" (one of his favorite phrases), he did succeed in making the White House safe for culture. The Presidency became a focus for something more than politics.

A great deal of this *ton* is described in the paperback reissue of William Manchester's *Portrait of a President,* certainly the most entertaining of the Kennedy books. The President seemed to lend himself to this sort of exploitation easily, as though he had no real sense of privacy, or even propriety—an impression that was usually dispelled with a flash of Kennedy wit, used not so much against his foes, but to disarm his friends, who often needed disarming to go the whole way with him.

The wit (one volume just published consists of nothing but humorous remarks taken from speeches and press conferences) complemented the Kennedy "style"—and, among other things, allowed him to be an intellectual without acting like one. Benjamin Bradlee, for example, in *That Special Grace,* tells us that he could eat "ten bowls of specially prepared clam chowder without succumbing to either indigestion or embarrassment." (Human and yet how superhuman!—a real contribution to mythmaking.)

This is the necessary myth which, in a democracy, must expose the man before the official can be honored. Every American President has played the role, whether it be Hoover fishing or Eisenhower on the golf course. Yet we know that nothing is more fleeting than a reputation based on this kind of anecdotal small talk. The fresh and vibrant memories of Kennedy are already fading. A new man sits in the driver's seat; a First Lady gives way to a First Lady Bird; John-John will grow up, and I hope he never reads *Once There Was a President,* the picture album written about his life in the big White House.

The real contribution these books make, aside from their immediate appeal to a bereaved nation, is to provide an eye-bank for historians. If I had to choose but one among them, it would be *The Burden and the Glory*. It can be argued that these speeches were "ghosted," as, indeed, they were. But this is not to say that they are any the less his own—the man picks the writers who will best represent him, and Kennedy's philosophy pervades them all.

Yet, even here, history failed Kennedy, and we are glad it did. A nation whose revolution is technological ill serves the speechmaker. The President was constantly having to talk about "administratively induced stimulants to our economy," "declining mass transit systems," "output per man hour," and "liberalized depreciation guidelines." (It is President Johnson who has restored the simple word "poverty" to our vocabulary, in place of "surplus labor areas.")

The best speeches deal with the issues that weigh on us most heavily: nuclear testing, the United Nations, the Alliance for Progress, the search for peace. In these, Kennedy assumed the very mandate of humanity. "No problem of human destiny is beyond human beings," he stated in "What Kind of Peace Do We Want?" "Man's reason and spirit have often solved the seemingly unsolvable, and we believe they can do it again."

Over and over again in this book we sense the extent to which the President was determined to solve "with reason and spirit" the terrifying, irrational problems that threaten us. He did not always succeed. His judgments sometimes failed him, and the unfinished business of America was far from finished when he died. But his vision did not fail. It persists in these speeches, to give us the man who gave soul to the office, who will survive his legend—the Kennedy, in my opinion, who is worth preserving most.

### Clifton Fadiman

Mr. Fadiman has a quantity and quality reputation based on both electronic and printed journalism. He was for years master of ceremonies of the "Information Please" radio program and for a decade book editor of *The New Yorker*. Before that, he was an editor for Simon and Schuster, and for the past several years has been a member of the editorial board of the Book-of-the-Month Club. This review* originally appeared in the Book-of-the-Month Club *News*.

LIFE WITH PICASSO. By Françoise Gilot and Carlton Lake. New York: McGraw-Hill Book Company.

To help make this book unique several circumstances happily converge. First, the subject: Pablo Picasso is generally recognized as the preeminently versatile artist of our century, and may in perspective loom up as one of the greatest in the history of the West. Second, among his dazzling talents is that genius for self-exhibition which has made him a natural object of curiosity to vast audiences claiming no obsessive interest in modern art. Like Chaplin, de Gaulle or Churchill, he is one of the salient personalities of our epoch. Third, the book appears at a time when many Americans are discovering the deep satisfactions and pleasures offered by contemporary painting and sculpture at its finest. Fourth, Françoise Gilot, Picasso's mistress for ten years and the mother of Claude and Paloma, two of his children, chances to be not only an intelligent artist in her own right but also a biographer of true Boswellian blood, gifted with wit, a superb journalistic memory and—in view of the weird nature of her relations with Picasso—detachment sufficient to permit her book to be a convincing portrait and not a mere *chronique scandaleuse*. Finally, in Carlton Lake she has found a skillful collaborator to whom presumably we must assign much of the credit for the supple, rapid and charming English that clothes the story.

Françoise Gilot met Picasso in May, 1943, during the Nazi Occupation of France. She was 21, he more than forty years her senior, having been born in 1881. He was attracted by her youth (apparently he cannot tolerate women of his

* Reprinted by permission of Clifton Fadiman and The Book-of-the-Month Club *News*.

own generation), her intelligence, her talent and a certain mental consanguinity. She was attracted by—Picasso. They became lovers, in time she came to live with him in his fantastic household, they learned much from each other, she bore him children, in the end his overweening egotism was too much for her, she left him. She is now remarried, as is Picasso (to the youthful Jacqueline Rocque).

The book is thus a candid (yet perfectly well-bred) record of one of the important affairs in Picasso's rather active love life. It is a record set down with only an occasional touch of self-defensiveness and here and there an amusing overlay of malicious wit. But it is not primarily the personal story of a woman who loved a man, suffered through him, perhaps made him suffer too, and left him. It is intended to be, and is, a full-length portrait, painted with the knowledge that comes only from absolute intimacy, of a fascinating monster, a geyser of energy, a complex character whose ineffable egoism makes up merely one outstanding trait—and a very great artist. Especially the last. How fortunate we would feel if we possessed such a verbal portrait of Leonardo, Rembrandt or Michelangelo, depicted in their slippers and dressing gowns rather than as pedestaled historical figures.

But, though the most brilliant light plays on Picasso himself, we are also given a fine view of a whole generation of artists, or rather of two generations. By means of priceless anecdotes, told with Gallic wit and neatness, we are shown pictures of Malraux, Cocteau, Matisse, Hemingway (who once brought Picasso a house-gift of hand grenades), Gertrude Stein, Braque, Paul Eluard, Giacometti, Gide, Aragon, Chagall, Léger, Chaplin—the list is almost endless. A good example of Picasso's astounding self-revelatory statements is his explanation of his affair with the wife of his friend Eluard: "I only did it to make him happy. I didn't want him to think I didn't like his wife."

Picasso emerges, first of all, as a great talker. He must be
çoise Gilot he appears to have found a recording mechanism
one of the most articulate artists in history; and in Fran-

of genius. Supremely egotistical, he does not allow his vanity to interfere with his comprehension of his own work and destiny. He says of God: "God is really only another artist. He invented the giraffe, the elephant, and the cat. He has no real style. He just keeps on trying other things"; and we feel that he is thinking of himself, in both pride and humility. No one, probably, has ever explained Picasso better than he explains himself: "Reality must be torn apart in every sense of the word. What people forget is that everything is unique. Nature never produces the same thing twice." His understanding of himself is linked to an equally intuitive understanding of the time that produced him. "Strangeness was what we wanted to make people think about because we were quite aware that our world was becoming very strange and not exactly reassuring."

One of the high values of this book is the insight it gives us into the concrete life of the artist; it is felt from the inside. Mlle. Gilot writes like the painter she is: she sees first, then thinks, then at last puts down the words. The result is a book with a professional stance, quite unlike the usual remote or academic or romanticized "life" of an artist. The reader feels that he is in Picasso's studio, and at times even in Picasso's mind.

For Picasso the artist Mlle. Gilot has all possible admiration. For Picasso the lover and the man her admiration is qualified. "For me there are only two kinds of women—goddesses and doormats," states Picasso; and the paranoid attitude lying behind the words has made it difficult for Picasso to be happy with any of the women with whom he has lived. The necessity to dominate has made him hesitate to relinquish any of his relationships; so that Mlle. Gilot was forced to endure the continual reappearance into their joint life of his wife and former mistresses. The encounters thus produced were often extremely comic, and Mlle. Gilot, who has a dry humor, makes the most of them. But in the end the obligation to take on Picasso's past as well as Picasso himself was too much for her. Her final judgment points to the tragic failure implicit in the life of this triumphantly successful man: "On the path he travels, he goes alone and . . . his solitude is, as a result, unchangeable."

It is difficult to like this strange figure who sacrifices everyone in his path, for whom life "is a game one plays with no holds barred." It is clear that such magnificent off-beat geniuses as Picasso should never by law be allowed to become husbands or fathers: they have no talent for either role. But after one has made that conventional judgment, one feels that one has hardly diminished Picasso's stature. Selfish, stingy, erratic, cruel, often foolish he may be; none-theless from these pages emerges a human being who fills us with a sense of the potentialities of man. Picasso seems to live more in a day than most of us do in our lifetime. The miracle of the creative imagination is an abstract phrase. In this long, astonishing, crowded, intimate record the authors contrive to give it blood and bone and sinew.

## Harry Hansen

Mr. Hansen has long been a favorite of those who like a review which provides an adequate picture and appraisal of a book (which is not necessarily an indirect criticism of reviewers who use a new book as a springboard for an essay on some subject suggested by the book, because some of these pieces are quite entertaining and edifying, even though they do not tell us as much about the book as a good review should). Mr. Hansen has had a variety of newspaper and writing experiences. He has been a reporter and book reviewer for several newspapers and magazines (he conducted the book department for *Harper's Magazine* for over fifteen years), and was editor of the *O. Henry Prize Stories* for eight years. The author of several books, including *The Chicago* in the "Rivers of America" series, Mr. Hansen has also been lecturer on book reviewing in the Graduate School of Journalism at Columbia. This review* first appeared in the *Saturday Review*.

LETTERS FROM BOHEMIA. By Ben Hecht. New York: Doubleday & Company, Inc.

In the final year of Ben Hecht's life he turned once more to memories of the good fellowship he had enjoyed with a group of talented, erratic, and sometimes zany men who, he says, filled a full half of his life. His memories were sharpened because, in dying, these friends had deprived him of something; they "took with them part of my bloom. I felt more lessened than mournful." But the marked difference about these "stormy old friends" was their silence. "For a while an echo stays in your ear. You hear a laugh, a knowing phrase or two, a certain quality of enunciation. Then nothing. Another death takes place—voices. This is the technique of mortality—everything must vanish to make way for new things." And he mused: "You begin to look on mortality as a practical joke. . . ."

*Letters from Bohemia* describes Gene Fowler, H. L. Mencken, Sherwood Anderson, Maxwell Bodenheim, George Grosz, George Antheil, and Charles MacArthur. Reproduced are a number of their letters, mostly gossipy; only those by Antheil contain any valuable self-revelation. The book is bizarre entertainment, chiefly an exhibit in the mutations of reminiscence. For Ben has described most of these friends, or told these anecdotes, many times. His formal autobiography, *A Child of the Century,* is full of them. MacArthur is in *Charlie,* and Ben's newspaper days in Chicago are relived in *Gaily, Gaily.* No man ever wrote or talked with such gusto about multitudes of experiences as Ben.

This retelling is a trait of the true raconteur—and Ben Hecht was one of the best. He was a genuine storyteller in

* Reprinted by permission of Harry Hansen and the *Saturday Review.*

print and in speech, for he was fluent in both, and his feeling for the dramatic, the unconventional, the ironies in human behavior gave vitality to his tales. His invention needed only a few artifacts to start operating. He could organize his material to suit a newspaper column, a television interview, a scenario, or a play. Although he professed to despise popular taste, he took pride in completed work in any media. Well-balanced himself, he took great enjoyment in the antics of his unregimented, convivial associates.

The portrait of George Antheil is to me the most engrossing, partly because it shows Hecht at his best in taking the measure of a man. Hecht admired Antheil's tremendous energy, restless ambition, and immense self-assurance. Antheil fought the piano as if it were an enemy:

"Music poured out of Antheil sixteen hours a day. He did nothing but write music and play it on the piano, which he made sound like a calliope in a circus parade. . . . At home or in hotel suites, Georgie played the piano until his swollen fingers had to be stuck in a bowl of ice for healing. As he played the piano, pummeling the hell out of its keys and stomping on the loud pedal, Georgie sang the various instrumental parts of his compositions. His half-falsetto squeal supplied horn, fiddle, flute and drum accompaniments. I listened always with fascination to Antheil's more splintery compositions. They were as unsoothing as a punch on the nose."

Antheil is the central character of an anecdote that is an excellent example of Hecht's technique. It belongs somewhere between Bemelmans and O. Henry, and is right out of the *Thousand and One Afternoons*. Hecht and Herman Mankiewicz, toiling in Hollywood and stuffed with money, conspired with Antheil to give a dinner for twelve ladies of the ballet, who in turn would dance only for them, with Antheil at the piano. The story embodies Hecht's fluid style, his easy way with improbabilities, his touch of exaggeration and his gift of caricature.

Of Sherwood Anderson, Hecht recalled best his immense self-love. Anderson "never tried to please anybody. He considered it everybody's duty to please him." Hecht wondered why Anderson boasted of his faults. "You couldn't tell whether he was lying or telling the truth when he spoke of himself. He seemed to be lying, but why should a man lie about being a cruel and deceitful fellow if he wasn't?" Although he concludes that Anderson was a likable man ("He had the charm of indifference."), Hecht proves that Anderson was a self-serving, grossly calculating person by recalling the latter's behavior to several women who had confidence in him, one of whom later jumped her horse off a cliff.

The Bodenheim legend is largely the creation of Hecht, who wrote endlessly about him. The two men were briefly associated in editing the untrammeled Chicago *Literary Times,* after which Bodenheim was intermittently a target for Hecht's wit. "Bogie's" comments were sometimes brilliant, but he dipped his pen in acid, and for any form of conventional living he had an undisguised contempt, which seemed to extend even to his own person. The appended letters are mostly appeals for handouts. But the memoir, though frank about Bodenheim's shortcomings, is generous in tone and the best portrait posterity is likely to have of a gifted man whose compulsions destroyed him.

As a youthful reporter, Ben Hecht gave H. L. Mencken wide-eyed adulation. Mencken in turn recognized the lad's inventiveness and put him to work writing short stories for the Mencken-Nathan *Smart Set*. Ben said he paid "convict prices" (around $40) and "was pleased by the fact that I didn't mind his signing pseudonyms to my stories."

Gene Fowler had a solid reputation as an executive of three New York newspapers, and as author of novels and topical biographies. Hecht thinks Fowler's excessive modesty kept him from writing about himself, but it is evident that Gene circulated plenty of personal anecdotes among his friends. Hecht repeats the story of Fowler cruising around the country with a corpse in tow, the itinerary somewhat expanded since the last telling. The tale that Fowler, crossed in love, walked on a two-foot ledge around the tenth story of a hotel rests solely on Fowler's assertion. Also a bit hard for a literalist to take is the yarn that Fowler, ordered to print a four-page dummy of Hearst's prospective *Daily Mirror,* filled the pages with outrageous fictive boudoir exploits of the owner, who reacted only mildly. Hecht writes that Fowler was intractable when in his cups, but he was cold sober when he threw his office furniture out a window because the Hollywood studio manager refused to install a couch.

The sketch of George Grosz is brief and that of Charles MacArthur is reminiscent of earlier writings. Like everyone else, Ben was under the spell of Charlie's amiable and impish character, and he explains their collaboration: "I needed somebody else's love for the stage as a stimulant."

The tremendous energy of Hecht's associates, whether well used or misdirected, has ceased. They indulge no more in their "talent for ridiculing life," in their "genius for distaste." They did not survive to write Ben's epitaph, but he has provided plenty of proof that theirs embodies his own.

CHARLES ALVA HOYT

Mr. Hoyt is a member of the English faculty of Bennett College, Millbrook, New York. More important, however, for purposes of this book is what he teaches through the following example about book reviewing. In the language of Mrs. Barry Bingham, editor, The World of Books, Louisville (Ky.) *Courier-Journal,* in which paper this review appeared:

"It seems to me that his review of Peter Matthiessen's *At Play in the Fields of the Lord* evinces some of the qualities which a good book review ought to have: it suggests the subject of the book without embarking on a dogged and interest-destroying resume of the plot; it brings to bear upon the book critical acumen in an ambience of hospitality and warmth, untouched by smart aleckness; it sparks in the reader an interest in the book, even a desire to read it."

AT PLAY IN THE FIELDS OF THE LORD. By Peter Matthiessen. 375 pp. Random House. $5.95.

*The reason Milton wrote in fetters when he wrote of Angels and God, and at liberty when of Devils and Hell, is because he was a true Poet and of the devil's party without knowing it.*

This opinion, so galling to professional Miltonians, is to be found in William Blake's "The Marriage of Heaven and Hell." It finally occurred to me as an apt embodiment of my discomfort at portions of this brilliant novel by Peter Matthiessen. The book has attracted considerable critical attention already, most of which is directed toward those parts of it which describe the efforts of the American adventurer, half-breed and professional no-account, Lewis Moon, to found a new Indian resistance in the Amazon jungles. True, these parts are engrossing, but they do not introduce us to the novel. That job Mr. Matthiessen entrusts to another plot section, that dealing with the expedition of a family of Protestant missionaries from the American Midwest. These people are at once so pathetic and so obnoxious that for many pages I could not accept them, but Mr. Matthiessen ends by convincing me. At least he has me believing that if there are no such creatures, it is necessary to invent them.

"The Marriage of Heaven and Hell" would in fact make an excellent subtitle for this book, which is of a great tradition: the civilization-vs.-barbarity, man-against-the-jungle epics. Like some of the best of them, it does not care to take sides in the fight. Civilization is here represented by such figures as Commandante Guzman, who hopes to stir up an incident as a pretext for exterminating a whole tribe of Indians; and Les Huben, a missionary right out of Elmer Gantry, and a rare hand at the parochial letter:

"The devil has inflicted a heavy defeat on the forces of God. Pray much for the soul of Martin Quarrier, slain by the savages; pray much for the soul of our young ambassador-in-Jesus, Billy Quarrier, deceased only a short span before his dad . . . and by the way, I want to thank all of my friends in Christ for that fine new outboard motor—it's a beaut!"

The Indians themselves are not superior beings, but savages, uncomprehending, proud and violent.

The novel is beautifully constructed. Like *Heart of Darkness,* it shows us the absolutely unrelenting enemy of civilized decency and cleanliness that is the jungle itself—a vast trust of wilderness which acts to elevate one character and debase the next. Lewis Moon had a great future, but couldn't escape his half-breed status. A drunk and a traitor to all those who had faith in him, he finally finds a cause in the forest among the primitive Niaruna people. He has escaped civilization at last. On the other hand the Quarriers and the Hubens, those brash supersalesmen of the Zenith Christ, find nothing but resistance, confusion and death, all of which they have richly deserved, if only for their dialect—"Jumping Jehoshaphat!" Hazel cried . . . Of course, by the end of the book Matthiessen has us feeling sorry even for these, and I daresay that is how he manages to make us believe in them. Personally, I didn't think it could be done.

*At Play in the Fields of the Lord* is a book, then, full of matter and portent—I can see it on college reading lists in a year or so. Before it is thus embalmed, however, I hope it gets a good hearing from the community at large, because it is both exciting and thought-provoking, a thoroughly worthwhile book.

Here is a brief review of the same book from *The Virginia Quarterly Review:*

AT PLAY IN THE FIELDS OF THE LORD. By Peter Matthiessen.

Two dedicated missionaries and their wives, plus one no less dedicated adventurer and soldier of fortune, each intent on bringing religion, salvation, and civilization to a band of savages along one of the tributaries of the upper Amazon River, find instead disappointment, disillusionment, and death at the hands of Mr. Matthiessen, novelist turned naturalist and explorer, and now novelist once again. His relentless and merciless investigation of hopeless and fruitless careers no matter how oriented proves to be at once thorough and interesting, despite the fact that his characters tend to run off with him, just when his narrative seems to change direction and become a study of Good and Evil. Perhaps a shorter book would have strengthened the author's juxtaposition of the two, increased its effectiveness, and heightened its emotional impact, but his story is homily enough for a month of Sundays in any case. *Random $5.95*

JOSEPH HENRY JACKSON

As book editor of the San Francisco *Chronicle,* contributor to various magazines, and author of several books, Mr. Jackson was an outstanding literary personage of the west coast and of the country as a whole. This review* is from the *Chronicle.*

THE COMMON COLD AND HOW TO FIGHT IT. By Dr. Noah D. Fabricant. New York: Ziff-Davis Publishing Company.

Have you a cold?

If my own observation lately is accurate at all you probably have. There's a jolly little epidemic about—low-grade, fortunately—and practically everyone you know is sneezing and coughing.

Doubtless the Ziff-Davis Publishing Company has nothing

* Reprinted by permission of Joseph Henry Jackson and the San Francisco *Chronicle.*

to do with this, but things could hardly have fallen out more happily for that concern, which brings out this week a little book provocatively (under the circumstances) titled *The Common Cold and How to Fight It,* by Dr. Noah D. Fabricant. No magic formulas occupy space in the author's 100-page dissertation. The volume is merely a survey of what the medical profession knows—and doesn't know—today about the common cold.

Of all ailments the common cold is the most democratic, says Dr. Fabricant. No one is immune by virtue of his position or importance.

Curiously, however, the incidence of the common cold is greater among members of the lower income brackets. Why? The doctor doesn't analyze this; he merely makes the statement and lets it go at that. There is a good reason, however, and a simple one. General opinion among doctors is that those in higher income groups don't get colds as often partly because they eat better and hence keep in better physical condition, and partly because they don't mix so frequently with crowds. The "eat better," by the way, though it follows the income curve, doesn't necessarily depend upon more money. Your "hog-and-hominy" eater in the South could balance with greens if he knew enough; a vegetable patch 10 feet square isn't a matter of cash.

Just the same, only one person in four goes through the winter without at least one cold—high and low incomes alike.

Dr. Fabricant examines, first, not causes but predisposing factors. Sudden changes in temperature are among leading factors here, and the doctor explains the mechanics of this with diagrams of the upper respiratory tract. There are other such factors, too, and he lists and explains these—among them being the wrong kinds of "nose drops" which lower the capacity of man's natural protective mechanisms to protect him. Here, by the way, he has something to say about the fad for "alkalinizing," noting that while the healthy person's blood is slightly alkaline, the normal secretions of the nose, for example, are acid. He adds, "Most germs associated with acute upper respiratory diseases resent this normal acid environment and prefer an alkaline background for their growth and multiplication." That's a point worth thinking about.

Most of the doctor's book, however, is concerned with "cures." He goes over these, painstakingly demonstrating that "cold shots" have by no means been proved to have any effect whatever, that allergies play a part in predisposing the individual to colds, that drinking "lots of fruit juices" won't do you any harm, but won't do you any good either, that it has never been proved that cathartics improve the situation by one jot or tittle, that the sulfa compounds have yet to be shown to have any effect on the common cold.

In sum, the doctor's advice comes to this: The best thing you can do when you come down with a cold is to go to bed and stay there. Reason: It isn't half so much the "cold" that does the damage as it is the secondary infection following it, and if you keep warm and quiet this secondary infection won't get going as readily.

Further, in order to avoid the "cold" itself, avoid lowering your body temperature suddenly, keep dry feet (because wet feet are cold feet), keep your general health good, especially during those months when you're most likely to be exposed to unavoidable changes in temperature which you need to resist. In this connection, by the way, the doctor notes that even though you are bundled up well, the sudden exit into cold night air chills you by way of your breathing—a point which inevitably reminds one of the Mexican and Central American Indians of the highlands who always muffle their faces at night, breathing through their serapes so as not to inhale chilly air.

Perhaps this whole affair sounds disappointing. And if you read Doctor Fabricant's book hoping to find a miracle you'll be disappointed sure enough. But my own view is that the doctor is well worth reading, if only because he will help you to jettison a deckload of false ideas you may have been carrying on the subject of colds. At least the author tells you —with the best medical opinion behind him—what won't cure a cold. That's something.

## Herbert A. Kenny

Editor for the Arts and Book Editor of the Boston *Globe*, Herbert A. Kenny has been in the newspaper business for over thirty years. Mr. Kenny has written two book collections of poetry—*Twelve Birds* and *Suburban Man*—and numerous articles for magazines. The following review appeared in the Boston *Globe*.

MATTERHORN CENTENARY. By Sir Arnold Lunn, Rand McNally, Chicago, 354 pp., $5.95.
BETWEEN HEAVEN AND EARTH. By Gaston Rebuffat, Photographs by Pierre Tairraz, Oxford University Press, N. Y., 183 pp. quarto, $12.50.

" 'If I were to invent a new idolatry,' wrote Leslie Stephen, who left the church in which he had been ordained to write An Agnostic's Apology, 'I should prostrate myself not before bird or beast or ocean but before one of those mighty masses to which, in spite of all reason, it is impossible not to attribute some shadowy personality.' " Thus one paragraph by Sir Arnold Lunn in his "Matterhorn Centenary." For it was in 1865 that Edward Whymper led the first successful assault on the world's proto-peak. Monte Cervino, Mont Cervin, the Matterhorn. It was a triumph; it was a tragedy. Seven men reached the peak; three returned to Zermatt. The final assault had proved unexpectedly easy; a broken rope on the return plunged four to their deaths. Today, it is said, on a summer afternoon 150 persons may reach the peak on a given day.

Sir Arnold, the father of skiing in Europe, knows Switzerland well and mountain climbing well, and English even better. He has put together an excellent history of the Matterhorn and its triumphs and tragedies.

Gaston Rebuffat and Pierre Tairraz have produced a book of magnificent photographs and exciting text on Alpine climbing. The Matterhorn is here, to be sure, but here also is Rebuffat's first ascent of the South face of the Aiguille du Midi, the Grande Traverse of Mont Blanc and the Bonatti routes on the Drus, all with different companions.

Tairraz gives us eight pages in full color, 104 in monochrome. They provide us with all the majesty of the Alps, although there is a sublimity about the John Ruskin paintings in Sir Arnold's book that reduces the terror and heightens the beauty. But it is terror as well as beauty that men seek in this strangest of sports, which became a sport only after Whymper—no sportsman but closer to a fanatic and an unpleasing one—had stood on top of the Matterhorn.

These are the lands of Awe and it is not difficult to understand Stephen's inclination, nor does it come as a surprise that the first man to climb the peaks (the passes were climbed from necessity, the peaks from passion) was a priest; but it was Whymper who gave mountaineering to the world.

## Max Lerner

Author, teacher, journalist, Max Lerner is currently Professor of American Civilization and World Politics at Brandeis University where he was Dean of the Graduate School. Mr. Lerner does a three-times-a-week syndicated newspaper column which appears widely in this country and abroad; has been editor of *The Nation* and other publications; and has travelled as a journalist and scholar to almost every part of the world. His recent book, *America as a Civilization*, received wide acclaim, was a best seller, has been translated and published around the world, and is now available in a 2-volume paperback edition. His latest work is *The Age of the Overkill: A Preface to World Politics*. The following review* appeared in *Life* Magazine.

* Reprinted by permission of Max Lerner and *Life*.

MORNING AND NOON. By Dean Acheson. Houghton Mifflin Co., $6.00.

It takes a man wholly without sawdust stuffing to produce an unstuffy autobiography, especially if he is a political figure who has a chance to glorify his career triumphs and write an apologia for his blunders. In *Morning and Noon* Dean Acheson has the grace to side-step both these dangers and the wit to make his people and places come alive.

The *Morning* of his title refers mainly to his happy childhood in Middletown, Conn., where his father was an Episcopalian rector, and to an idyllic summer with ax and surveying instruments in the wilderness of Canada, helping to build the Canadian National Railroad. These sketches of youth's golden age are done with a nostalgic richness of mood and memory, their style one of hyperbole mixed with irony.

The twig was bent toward freedom—"the freedom of wild things, not knowing unison, whose discipline came from pains . . . externally . . . imposed" without a "lecture or a verdict of moral or social obloquy." The remark sheds light on why he virtually omits his school days, and perhaps on the source of his disagreement with F.D.R., who demanded complete surrender to the New Deal crusade, and of his well-known dislike for Dulles' compulsion to intertwine foreign policy with morality.

This is not an autobiography but some highly selected memories. In fact, except for that great summer in Canada it jumps from early boyhood to Washington, where he started his career as law clerk to Justice Brandeis.

The portraits will be the heart of the book for most readers. The Brandeis who emerges is not a Messianic liberal but a stern individualist who believed in the individual mind only, and who saw "great stupid institutions, growing larger and larger, fall across the way and crowd into the little space which the individual has."

It was an accident that Acheson became Brandeis' clerk and not Holmes's. Holmes—with his Civil War scars, his mustaches, his anecdotes, his mockery of absolutes, his dry sense of the limits of life and law, his verbal necromancy—was a natural for him, and in a handful of pages he emerges life size. So do the portraits of the rest of "Our Court," especially its extreme reactionary, Justice McReynolds. Here Acheson shows that he can be deadly and still remain sympathetic. He recalls that McReynolds' "rigid" views and passionate temper were "ingredients that could hardly do other than produce a Colonel Blimp of the Bench," but relates with friendly humor the time McReynolds' valet put out the wrong pants for a formal soiree.

There is, as one would expect from Acheson's serious falling out with Roosevelt over a gold crisis in 1933, and his resignation from the Treasury, an unflattering portrait of F.D.R. He saw him as a man who "exuded a relish for power and command," but also as surfacy, slippery and devious: "his responses seemed too quick; his reasons too facile." The use of nicknames in his inner circle Acheson found "patronizing and humiliating."

But there is a rollicking account of the reconciliation that followed the Senate hearings on Frankfurter's appointment to the Supreme Court (at which Acheson had represented him as unofficial counsel). After Frankfurter had routed the badgering McCarran, there was a scene of high comedy in Senator Ashurst's office where they drank chilled brandy, and Frankfurter and Ashurst discovered a common passion for the post-Civil War romance of Senator Roscoe Conkling and Kate Chase, daughter of Lincoln's Secretary of the Treasury. "Let's see the President," said Frankfurter. "He'll love this story."

After six years, Acheson's fight with Roosevelt was over and he was in on the high strategy of 1940, writing the first draft of the "We have just begun to fight" speech. The book ends with his appointment as an Assistant Secretary of State in 1941.

The book's prime appeal is style—the style of a man's personality flawlessly reflected in his verbal style. There is an antiseptic and deflationary strain, as there is in the man, for anything too high-flown. There is little dogma in him, liberal or conservative, as there is little moralism. If it is a paean to anything, it is to the life of the law, and in his insider's memories of the Court he writes of what he knew and lived as a pro. If I had a son whom I wished to turn toward a legal career mingled with politics, this is the book I'd give him.

### Amy Loveman

As associate editor of *The Saturday Review of Literature* and head of the editorial staff of Book-of-the-Month, Amy Loveman was always respected and admired in literary circles. This,* one of her shorter reviews, appeared in the Book-of-the-Month Club *News*.

TRY AND STOP ME. By Bennett Cerf. New York: Simon and Schuster.

If you want to know how Mrs. Swift, of Chicago, got her comeuppance at the hands of Beatrice Lillie, or how Dorothy Parker turned the tables neatly against the supercilious lady who stood back to make way for her, exclaiming, "Age before beauty," or what Liddell Hart said to Bernard Shaw and Bernard Shaw said to Liddell Hart, or the formula that H. L. Mencken has evolved for answering controversial letters, or what Mr. Cerf thinks of Alexander Woollcott (and he doesn't think much), or of Gertrude Stein, or of Heywood Broun, or of a variety of other celebrities, here's your chance. After dinner speakers, editors in search of fillers, dinner guests in search of a laugh, let alone doctors' and dentists' offices, and the general reader wishing a pleasant book to beguile an idle quarter hour, will find this volume a veritable treasure house for their purposes. In it are collected stories, bons mots, repartee, gossip of all sorts, vignettes of well-known persons, and anecdotes of men and women connected with the theatre, the movies, publishing, café society, etc., arranged in loose classifications, and illustrated with car-

* Reprinted by permission of Amy Loveman and Book-of-the-Month Club *News*.

toons and drawings by Carl Rose. Interspersed among the snippets and anecdotes are longer pieces, and there is a great deal of informal characterization and comment. A perfect book to have beside the bed, or on the table to entertain the visitors who may have to turn to their own devices while the cocktails are being mixed. And a good antidote for a gloomy day.

### Orville Prescott

The reviewer in this instance is one of the conductors of "Books of the Times" in the daily New York *Times*. Mr. Prescott is the author of *In My Opinion: An Inquiry into the Contemporary Novel,* a volume of value to those concerned with reviewing. It has been said that Mr. Prescott's reviews are read by more people in the U.S.A. than those of any other single reviewer. Here is a review* of a book that was later to be awarded the 1965 Pulitzer Prize for fiction.

THE KEEPERS OF THE HOUSE. By Shirley Ann Grau. 310 pages. Knopf. $4.95.

Like a river rising in a swamp, which coils and meanders with leisurely and sluggish indifference, whose current flows so smoothly and steadily that its gradually increasing pace is unnoticed until the roar of the falls can be heard, Shirley Ann Grau's third novel, "The Keepers of the House," moves forward from the evocation of a mood and a local atmosphere to a climax of disaster and melodrama. Once again, as in a hundred less artfully written novels, the sounds and smells and folkways of the Deep South are conjured up and the onerous burden of the South's heritage of violence and of racial neurosis is dramatized in the lives of a few unhappy people. It is all an old and familiar story, but seldom has it been told so well. This is a novel of dignity, stature, compassion. But the feeling it generates is one of austere pity for the sorrows of mortals who insist on acting foolishly and sinfully, not the vicarious identification and warm sympathy aroused by concern for particular individuals.

The best fiction now being written about the South is the work of women, notably Elizabeth Spencer, Ellen Douglas and Shirley Ann Grau. Miss Grau's specialty seems to be the creation of a special world compounded in equal parts of exact observation and of imaginative creation. Lured into her pages by the unstudied beauty of her prose, one is soon immersed in the atmosphere of a remote and primitive land where the rhythms of nature and the cycle of the weather and the seasons serve as the background for violent deeds and elemental passions. The air is still with tension and it seems almost as if, in spite of her factual realism, Miss Grau were retelling a myth about life in a distant past.

"The Keepers of the House" is divided into three parts. The first is devoted to William Howland, a rich widower—big, heavy, bald and kind. One of his ancestors came out of the Tennessee hills to help Andy Jackson fight the British at New Orleans and never went home again. He settled in Wade County somewhere in the center of a state just like Alabama, and farmed and fought Indians and reared children. Other Howlands prospered until "a real Howland" meant "the best blood in the county, best land and most money." William Howland was born about 1880 (the chronology is uncertain), married, fathered a daughter and lost his wife. The last 30 years of his life he spent with a Negro mistress.

Howland's loyal affection for Margaret Carmichael was the most important thing in his life. A lonely trip he made into the depths of Honey Island Swamp is the best-described episode in "The Keepers of the House," a marvel of suggestive writing.

Margaret was only 18 when she moved into Howland's house. Her story takes up the second part of Miss Grau's book. Margaret was big and strong and ignorant, a lonely orphan brooding over life and death, communing with ghosts, her mind groping to understand everything—wild creatures and plants, white people and the lot of the Negro in the South. Good, patient, humble and brave, Margaret is the real heroine of "The Keepers of the House."

The narrator (if not heroine) of the last third of the novel is Howland's granddaughter, Abigail, a modern young woman brought up by Margaret along with Margaret's three children by Howland. Abigail's life as a Howland heiress and the wife of a cynical opportunist turned segregationist politician was hard. It became harder still when politics and racial fanaticism broke over her head in a dreadful storm. Her violent reaction may seem grotesquely exaggerated, but it brings "The Keepers of the House" to a fine climax.

Long after its plot and even its characters are forgotten, the brooding atmosphere of Shirley Ann Grau's beautifully written novel will linger in her readers' minds.

## John S. Sherman

Mr. Sherman is book and arts critic of the Sunday Minneapolis *Tribune* and Minneapolis *Star,* with which he has been connected since the early 1930's. He is author of *Music and Maestros: The Story of the Minneapolis Symphony Orchestra, Sunday Best: Collected Essays,* etc. The following review appeared in the Sunday Minneapolis *Tribune.*

DREISER. By W. A. Swanberg. Scribner's, 614 pages, $10.

Big writers have often enough been big fools, but rarely to the degree achieved by America's pioneering realist, Theodore Dreiser, as revealed in this comprehensive and exactingly documented biography by St. Paul author W. A. Swanberg.

The book compares with Mark Schorer's almost day-by-day account of Sinclair Lewis' life, both in forbidding length and its close, deadpan scrutiny of a gifted though fallible human being. Swanberg turns a flat, white light on Dreiser's doings and character, his towering egoism and often petty mind, suggests but does not probe the mystery of a creative power that transcended a fumbling technique.

What emerges from this immensely detailed chronicle is the figure of a megalomaniac with little self-knowledge, a man both gullible and suspicious, muddled in his mental processes, a bundle of feelings often contradictory and rarely controlled.

Dreiser never really learned to write—H. L. Mencken once said "he can't write, but nevertheless he is a great writer"—and his books, even when ruthlessly cut and edited, were wildernesses of plodding and graceless prose.

Yet he wrote "Sister Carrie," which demolished the prevailing gentility of American letters in its time, and "An American Tragedy," a novel that moved like a heavy juggernaut to its fateful finale, dragging the reader through a searing and unforgettable experience.

If Dreiser had been a decorous and well-behaved citizen, lacking the sense of compassion possessed only by a few, he could hardly have imagined or executed these American epics.

Yet these, and his lesser writings and much trash, came from a strange and rather unlovely character almost devoid of the instinct of gratitude, tricky in his business dealings, callous toward the literally scores of women in his life.

His second marriage, long delayed, was to a long-time mistress, whose slavish devotion he held lightly. He obsessively hunted willing females all his life, an insatiable satyr in his restless search and conquest of new loves. These furtive enterprises he defended by his fatalist theories of man as a mere pawn of "chemic" forces, which he linked with the larger concept of life as senseless and purposeless.

Biographer Swanberg has gone through a mountain of research to portray vividly this hulking man with protruding teeth and wall eye, forever folding and unfolding his pocket handkerchief, growing ever more omniscient and touchy as age came upon him. Toward the end he all but lost his novelist's gift as he angrily espoused various worthy causes and reforms, advocating yet distrusting communism, and frittering away his energies in pamphleteering and trysts with hero-worshipping girls.

This is candid portraiture, much of it stemming from Dreiser's candor but much also derived by poking into hitherto secret spots.

His life and his writings were closely intertwined, with one explaining the other, so this enterprise is no mere debunking exercise. But the Dreiser fans, of whom I have been one in the past, are in for a shock: Dreiser may have been a genius but he was also phenomenally stupid. Apparently, in our heroes, we can't have everything.

## Stanley Walker

Stanley Walker is best known, perhaps, for his *City Editor* and for the fact that he was once city editor of the New York *Herald Tribune*. Mr. Walker did a good deal of book reviewing for the Sunday book section of the *Herald Tribune* and contributed to various magazines. The following review* appeared in *The New Yorker* and has been chosen because it is unusual and clever.

WEBSTER'S BIOGRAPHICAL DICTIONARY. Springfield, Mass.: G. and C. Merriam Company.

(*Some puzzled reflections caused by an examination of the new Webster's Biographical Dictionary, published by the G. & C. Merriam Company, Springfield, Mass., edited by Dr. William Allan Neilson, and containing more than forty thousand names, from Svend Aagesen, Danish historian, to Huldreich Zwingli, a Swiss religious reformer who lived from 1484 to 1531. Price, $6.50.*)

Dr. Neilson, after your biography of Noah Webster, lexicographer,

You warn, "Do not confuse Noah Webster with Daniel Webster."
And when you have finished with Daniel Webster, statesman,
You say, "Do not confuse Daniel Webster with Noah Webster."
Very well, Doctor, we shall not confuse them; we never have.
But may we speak with you upon the subject of confusion?
Your employers, the Merriam people, are good at words,
But when they tackle biography they enter a tricky field
Strewn with no end of dangerous editorial booby traps.

You sought to pick out forty thousand notables, living and dead,
And embalm them in a sort of all-time, all-embracing *Who's Who.*
You have had help: Dr. Nabih Amin Faris on the Arabic stuff,
Dr. Heinz A. Wieschhoff on the bewildering Bantu material,
And Dr. Morris Swadesh to check on the Aztec riddles.

Mind you, the result is far from bad, but, sadly, not foolproof.
An admirable range—Nicholas Murray Butler and Semiramis,
Paul Robeson and Prester John, Moses and Gene Buck.
And it's good to know that Tipoo Tib was the nickname
Of Hamidi bin Muhammad, slave trader in equatorial Africa,
And that Garet Garrett's real name is Edward Peter Garrett,
And that Geronimo in late life joined the Dutch Reformed Church,
And that Babe Ruth's name is pronounced the familiar way.
You say the selections and omissions were free from bias.
Is that so? Look closely, Doctor—are you sure of that?

Why did you blackball Payne Whitney, who died May 25, 1927,

And left a net estate of $178,893,655? Wasn't that enough?
Yet you include his brother, Harry Payne Whitney, who left less.

Moreover, in pugilism you are all on the side of the big men;
You have Sullivan, Corbett, Jeffries, Johnson, Willard,
Dempsey and Tunney and Schmeling—all heavyweights.
But where are the others? Gans, the Old Master, is out. So are
Bat Nelson, the Durable Dane; Greb, the Pittsburgh Windmill;
Ketchel, the Michigan Assassin; Wilde, the Mighty Atom;
Wolgast, the Cadillac Wildcat; and Walker, the Toy Bulldog.
They weren't heavy enough for you, eh, Dr. Neilson?

Among outlaws you have Jesse James and Cole Younger.
Good stuff, but why snub good old Frank James,
In many ways a better man than his tragic brother, Jesse?
You give a place to that sneering little rat, Billy the Kid,
But not a word for Pat Garrett, the sheriff who killed him
One night in Pete Maxwell's house in New Mexico in 1881.

You have some Gimbels, from Jacob to Bernard F.,
But who, if anybody, was R. H. Macy? You don't say.
You list Samuel Colt, six-shooter inventor, and Stetson,
Who made the famous hat, but nowhere do you say
That Sam Glidden of DeKalb, Ill., perfected barbed wire.
You set down many a pip-squeak journalist, but somehow
Fremont Older, the lion of the Pacific Coast, is out.
And why isn't W. Averell Harriman in your 40,000 Club?
You have Martial (Marcus Valerius Martialis), epigrammatist,
Who flourished back in the first century, but Wilson Mizner
Is out in the cold. Not because he drank, we trust?
Also, why couldn't Alphonse Capone make the grade?

And did you, perchance, never hear of Lt. Com. Walter Winchell?
He's out, but in are O. O. McIntyre and Westbrook Pegler,
And so is Lucius Beebe, listed as an "American journalist,"
Author of "Fallen Stars" (1921), but with no mention
Of his clothes or his mastery of basic pidgin.

Speaking of confusion, Doctor, as we were, what now?
You say Big Bill Haywood was tried in 1907 on a charge
Of participating in the killing of a former Idaho governor,
"Frank R. Strunenberg." The name, sir, was Steunenberg.
Borah was prosecutor, with Clarence Darrow defending.
Again, referring to Abe Hummel, the crooked lawyer,
You say he lived his last years in "poverty and obscurity."
The truth is, Dr. Neilson, he lived quietly but well,
Bet on the horses in both England and France,
And left enough money to start a sensational lawsuit.

A minor matter, perhaps, Doctor, but what have you against
Clifton Fadiman? You say that Kieran, Levant, and Adams all
Appear on "Information Please"—but no Fadiman.

When you come to William Allen White (born 1868),
You say he's sometimes known as the Sage of Potato Hill.
No, Doctor, the one and only Potato Hill sage (1853-1937)
Was Ed Howe (Edgar Watson Howe), editor and paragrapher,
Who had a farm on the Missouri River called Potato Hill.
Also, what makes you think that Heber Jebediah Grant,
The bearded, thrifty Mormon leader, died in 1937?
Perhaps you should hire some new necrology experts.
Mr. Grant lived, at last word, on Eighth Avenue, Salt Lake City.

But remember, Dr. Neilson, be careful not to confuse
Daniel Webster with Noah Webster, or vice versa.

## Edward Weeks

Editor-in-Chief of *The Atlantic Monthly* for twenty-eight years, consultant and senior editor of The Atlantic Monthly Press, lecturer, scholar, author, and literary critic, Edward Weeks is noted for his distinguished *Atlantic* column, "The Peripatetic Reviewer." His books include *This Trade of Writing, In Friendly Candor, The Open Heart* and *Breaking into Print*—all of which may be read with profit by those interested in book reviewing. This review* is from *The Atlantic*.

DOROTHY AND RED. By Vincent Sheean. Boston: Houghton Mifflin Company.

When Dorothy Thompson and Sinclair Lewis met at a dinner party at her Berlin flat in July, 1927, the spark was instantaneous, and by the time coffee had been served, he had maneuvered her into a corner and asked her to marry him. "I don't even know you, Mr. Lewis," she said with a quick laugh. The party was to celebrate her thirty-third birthday; the heartbreak of her disastrous first marriage to an ersatz Hungarian poet was past. She was surrounded by friends, and was at her fresh and vibrant best. Lewis at forty-two was our most provocative novelist, a somewhat mangy lion who was seeking a divorce from his first wife, Grace Hegger, and who, despite the enormous success of his four big novels (*Elmer Gantry* had just been published), was drinking hard. On this particular evening he was on good behavior. He told Dorothy of an idyllic farm in Vermont where he would like to live and work, and the appeal of his eyes and words was irresistible. He was to go on proposing until at last she consented, and the story of their thirteen years together, of the attraction that held them until his

* Reprinted by permission of Edward Weeks and The Atlantic Monthly Co.

drinking bouts and the demands of her career started the inevitable separation, has been told with compassionate understanding by one of their closest friends, Vincent Sheean, in his volume of reminiscence with letters, *Dorothy and Red.*

A minister's daughter, Dorothy lived with "a sense of historic mission," and from the first she was determined that her marriage with Hal, as she preferred to call him, would be a creative one, even if it meant subordinating her own career. She brought to him a sympathy and an intellectual admiration which for a time appeased his stormy vulnerability. They did, indeed, find their Twin Farms in Vermont, but on everything to do with the running of the place, as Mr. Sheean points out, they were at odds. Dorothy was proud to bear him a child, yet somehow she never seemed to be able to keep young Michael and his boisterous friends from raising bedlam within Hal's hearing, and he had a very short temper with children. The house parties here and abroad, some of them stretching on for ten days, which in her extravagant way Dorothy engineered, sound ghastly to me, and Red would fling away from them drunk and disgusted. The publication of her book *I Saw Hitler* in 1931 led to her expulsion the following year from Nazi Germany; now she was an international celebrity, and her absorption in Central Europe, her prophetic warning of what was coming, her strenuous assignments, created longer and longer absences.

This book is full of the stress of living and warm with love. At the core of it are Dorothy's letters and journals, and at the end the account of her visit to Sauk Centre at the time of the Sinclair Lewis Celebration, an essay which originally appeared in this magazine, and surely the most touching epitaph that ever will be written about the troubled "Red."

# APPENDIX

A BOOK

*A book is like a pilgrimage of old*
*Whose mission was the shrines in ancient lands;*
*A book is but a caravan for gold*
*And spice and amber wines—for precious bands*
*Of ivory, more white and sleek than the breast*
*Of a swan. A book is travel and surprise,*
*As one might see the Nile who had not guessed*
*Its color—darker than the tempest-skies.*

*What else? A book is like the yellow spill*
*Of lamp-glow in the night—and like the warm,*
*Quick touch of a hand that pledges to fulfill*
*The promises of friends for times of storm.*
*Who has not lived with books has never known*
*The purple splendor of a reader's throne.*

—Walter Blackstock Jr.

## APPENDIX

This appendix consists of six items that should be of interest and help to readers of this book:

(1) The names of the winners of the Alfred B. Nobel Prizes for Literature.

(2) The names of the winners of the Pulitzer Prizes in Fiction, Poetry, Biography, History, General Non-fiction, and Drama.

(3) The names of the winners of the National Book Awards in Fiction, Non-fiction and Poetry.

(4) The names of the winners of the John Newbery Medal.

(5) The names of the winners of the Caldecott Medal.

(6) Comments on the use of quotations in book reviews.

*The Winners of the Alfred B. Nobel Prizes for Literature*

1901—R. F. A. Sully Prudhomme, French
1902—Th. Mommsen, German
1903—B. Björnson, Norwegian
1904—F. Mistral, French, and J. Echegaray, Spanish
1905—H. Sienkiewicz, Polish
1906—G. Carducci, Italian
1907—R. Kipling, English
1908—R. Eucken, German
1909—Selma Lagerlöf, Swedish (first woman)
1910—P. Heyse, German
1911—M. Maeterlinck, Belgian
1912—G. Hauptmann, German
1913—R. Tagore, Bengali
1914—No award
1915—Romain Rolland, French
1916—Verner von Heidenstam, Swedish

1917—K. Gjellerup and H. Pontoppidan, Danish
1918—No award
1919—Carl Spitteler, Swiss
1920—Knut Hamsun, Norwegian
1921—Anatole France, French
1922—J. Benavente, Spanish
1923—W. B. Yeats, Irish
1924—Wladyslaw Reymont, Polish
1925—G. B. Shaw, English
1926—Signora G. Deledda, Italian
1927—Henri Bergson, French
1928—Sigrid Undset, Norwegian
1929—Thomas Mann, German
1930—Sinclair Lewis, American
1931—Erik A. Karlfeldt, Swedish
1932—John Galsworthy, English
1933—Ivan Bunin, Russian
1934—Luigi Pirandello, Italian
1935—No award
1936—Eugene O'Neill, American
1937—Roger M. du Gard, French
1938—Pearl Buck, American
1939—Eemil Sillanpää, Finnish
1940—No award
1941—No award
1942—No award
1943—No award
1944—Johannes V. Jensen, Danish
1945—Gabriela Mistral (pseudonym of Lucila Godoy y Alcayaga), Chilean
1946—Hermann Hesse, Swiss
1947—André Gide, French
1948—T. S. Eliot, English
1949—William Faulkner, American
1950—Bertrand Russell, English
1951—Pär Lagerkvist, Swedish
1952—François Mauriac, French

1953—Winston Churchill, English
1954—Ernest Hemingway, American
1955—Halldór Laxness, Icelander
1956—J. R. Jimenez, Spanish
1957—Albert Camus, French
1958—Boris Pasternak, Russian (declined)
1959—Salvatore Quasimodo, Italian
1960—St.-John Perse (pseudonym of Aléxis Léger), French
1961—Ivo Andric, Yugoslavian
1962—John Steinbeck, American
1963—Giorgos Seferis (pseudonym of Giorgos Seferiades), Greek
1964—Jean Paul Sartre, French (declined)
1965—Mikhail Sholokhov, Russian

### *Pulitzer Prize Winners*

#### *Fiction*

1918—Ernest Poole, *His Family*
1919—Booth Tarkington, *The Magnificent Ambersons*
1920—No award
1921—Edith Wharton, *The Age of Innocence*
1922—Booth Tarkington, *Alice Adams*
1923—Willa Cather, *One of Ours*
1924—Margaret Wilson, *The Able McLaughlins*
1925—Edna Ferber, *So Big*
1926—Sinclair Lewis, *Arrowsmith* (declined)
1927—Louis Bromfield, *Early Autumn*
1928—Thornton Wilder, *The Bridge of San Luis Rey*
1929—Julia Peterkin, *Scarlet Sister Mary*
1930—Oliver La Farge, *Laughing Boy*
1931—Margaret Ayer Barnes, *Years of Grace*
1932—Pearl Buck, *The Good Earth*
1933—T. S. Stribling, *The Store*
1934—Caroline Miller, *Lamb in His Bosom*
1935—Josephine Winslow Johnson, *Now in November*
1936—H. L. Davis, *Honey in the Horn*

1937—Margaret Mitchell, *Gone with the Wind*
1938—John Phillips Marquand, *The Late George Apley*
1939—Marjorie Kinnan Rawlings, *The Yearling*
1940—John Steinbeck, *The Grapes of Wrath*
1941—No award
1942—Ellen Glasgow, *In This Our Life*
1943—Upton Sinclair, *Dragon's Teeth*
1944—Martin Flavin, *Journey in the Dark*
1945—John Hersey, *A Bell for Adano*
1946—No award
1947—Robert Penn Warren, *All the King's Men*
1948—James A. Michener, *Tales of the South Pacific*
1949—James Gould Cozzens, *Guard of Honor*
1950—A. B. Guthrie, Jr., *The Way West*
1951—Conrad Richter, *The Town*
1952—Herman Wouk, *The Caine Mutiny*
1953—Ernest Hemingway, *The Old Man and the Sea*
1954—No award
1955—William Faulkner, *A Fable*
1956—MacKinlay Kantor, *Andersonville*
1957—No award
1958—James Agee, *A Death in the Family*
1959—Robert Taylor, *Travels of Jamie McPheeters*
1960—Allen Drury, *Advise and Consent*
1961—Harper Lee, *To Kill a Mockingbird*
1962—Edwin O'Connor, *The Edge of Sadness*
1963—William Faulkner, *The Reivers*
1964—No award
1965—Shirley Ann Grau, *Keepers of the House*
1966—Katherine Anne Porter, *Collected Stories*

*Poetry*

1922—Edwin Arlington Robinson, *Collected Poems*
1923—Edna St. Vincent Millay, *The Ballad of the Harp-Weaver; A Few Figs from Thistles; Eight Sonnets*
1924—Robert Frost, *New Hampshire*
1925—Edwin Arlington Robinson, *Man Who Died Twice*

1926—Amy Lowell, *What's O'Clock?*
1927—Leonora Speyer, *Fiddler's Farewell*
1928—Edwin Arlington Robinson, *Tristram*
1929—Stephen Vincent Benét, *John Brown's Body*
1930—Conrad Aiken, *Selected Poems*
1931—Robert Frost, *Collected Poems*
1932—George Dillon, *The Flowering Stone*
1933—Archibald MacLeish, *Conquistador*
1934—Robert Hillyer, *Collected Verse*
1935—Audrey Wurdemann, *Bright Ambush*
1936—Robert P. Tristram Coffin, *Strange Holiness*
1937—Robert Frost, *A Further Range*
1938—Marya Zaturenska, *Cold Morning Sky*
1939—John Gould Fletcher, *Selected Poems*
1940—Mark Van Doren, *Collected Poems*
1941—Leonard Bacon, *Sunderland Capture*
1942—William Rose Benét, *The Dust Which Is God*
1943—Robert Frost, *A Witness Tree*
1944—Stephen Vincent Benét, *Western Star*
1945—Karl Shapiro, *V-Letter and Other Poems*
1946—No award
1947—Robert Lowell, *Lord Weary's Castle*
1948—W. H. Auden, *The Age of Anxiety*
1949—Peter Viereck, *Terror and Decorum*
1950—Gwendolyn Brooks, *Annie Allen*
1951—Carl Sandburg, *Complete Poems*
1952—Marianne Moore, *Collected Poems*
1953—Archibald MacLeish, *Collected Poems*
1954—Theodore Roethke, *The Waking*
1955—Wallace Stevens, *Collected Poems*
1956—Elizabeth Bishop, *Poems, North and South*
1957—Richard Wilbur, *Things of This World*
1958—Robert Penn Warren, *Promises: Poems 1954-1956*
1959—Stanley Kunitz, *Selected Poems: 1928-1958*
1960—W. D. Snodgrass, *Heart's Needle*
1961—Phyllis McGinley, *Times Three: Selected Verse from Three Decades*

1962—Alan Dugan, *Poems*
1963—William Carlos Williams, *Pictures from Breughel*
1964—Louis Simpson, *At the End of the Open Road*
1965—John Berryman, *Seventy-Seven Dream Songs*
1966—Richard Eberhart, *Selected Poems (1930-1965)*

*Biography, Autobiography*

1917—Laura E. Richards and Maude Howe Elliott, assisted by Florence Howe Hall, *Julia Ward Howe*
1918—William Cabell Bruce, *Benjamin Franklin Self-Revealed*
1919—Henry Adams (*post obitum*), *The Education of Henry Adams*
1920—Albert J. Beveridge, *The Life of John Marshall*
1921—Edward W. Bok, *The Americanization of Edward Bok*
1922—Hamlin Garland, *Daughter of the Middle Border*
1923—Burton J. Hendrick, *The Life and Letters of Walter Hines Page*
1924—Michael Pupin, *From Immigrant to Inventor*
1925—M. A. DeWolfe Howe, *Barrett Wendell and His Letters*
1926—Dr. Harvey Cushing, *Life of Sir William Osler*
1927—Emory Holloway, *Whitman*
1928—Charles Edward Russell, *The American Orchestra and Theodore Thomas*
1929—Burton J. Hendrick, *The Training of an American*
1930—Marquis James, *The Raven* (Biography of Sam Houston)
1931—Henry James, *Charles W. Eliot*
1932—Henry F. Pringle, *Theodore Roosevelt*
1933—Allan Nevins, *Grover Cleveland*
1934—Tyler Dennett, *John Hay*
1935—Douglas Southall Freeman, *Robert E. Lee*
1936—Ralph Barton Perry, *The Thought and Character of William James*

1937—Allan Nevins, *Hamilton Fish—The Inner History of the Great Administration*
1938—Odell Shepard, *Pedlar's Progress—The Life of Bronson Alcott* and Marquis James, *Andrew Jackson* (Volume One, *The Border Captain* and Volume Two, *Portrait of a President*)
1939—Carl Van Doren, *Benjamin Franklin*
1940—Ray Stannard Baker, *Woodrow Wilson, Life and Letters*
1941—Ola Elizabeth Winslow, *Jonathan Edwards*
1942—Forrest Wilson, *Crusader in Crinoline*
1943—Samuel Eliot Morison, *Admiral of the Ocean Sea*
1944—Carleton Mabee, *The American Leonardo: The Life of Samuel F. B. Morse*
1945—Russel Blaine Nye, *George Bancroft, Brahmin Rebel*
1946—Linnie Marsh Wolfe (*post obitum*), *Son of the Wilderness* (Biography of John Muir)
1947—William Allen White, *The Autobiography of William Allen White*
1948—Margaret Clapp, *Forgotten First Citizen: John Bigelow*
1949—Robert E. Sherwood, *Roosevelt and Hopkins*
1950—Samuel Flagg Bemis, *John Quincy Adams and the Foundations of American Foreign Policy*
1951—Margaret Lewis Coit, *John C. Calhoun: American Portrait*
1952—Merlo J. Pusey, *Charles Evans Hughes*
1953—David J. Mays, *Edmund Pendleton 1721-1803*
1954—Charles A. Lindbergh, *The Spirit of St. Louis*
1955—William S. White, *The Taft Story*
1956—Talbot F. Hamlin, *Benjamin Henry Latrobe*
1957—John F. Kennedy, *Profiles in Courage*
1958—Douglass Southall Freeman (deceased 1953), *George Washington, Vols. I-VI;* John Alexander Carroll and Mary Wells Ashworth, *Vol. VII*
1959—Arthur Walworth, *Woodrow Wilson: American Prophet*

1960—Samuel Eliot Morison, *John Paul Jones*
1961—David Donald, *Charles Sumner and the Coming of the Civil War*
1962—No award
1963—Leon Edel, *Henry James: Vol. II, The Conquest of London, 1870-1881; Vol. III, The Middle Years, 1881-1895*
1964—Walter Jackson Bate, *John Keats*
1965—Dr. Ernest Samuels, *Henry Adams*
1966—Arthur M. Schlesinger, Jr., *A Thousand Days*

*History*

1917—J. J. Jusserand, *With Americans of Past and Present Days*
1918—James Ford Rhodes, *A History of the Civil War*
1919—No award
1920—Justin H. Smith, *The War with Mexico*
1921—Rear Admiral William Sowden Sims, *The Victory at Sea*
1922—James T. Adams, *The Founding of New England*
1923—Charles Warren, *The Supreme Court in United States History*
1924—Charles Howard McIlwain, *The American Revolution: A Constitutional Interpretation*
1925—Frederic L. Paxson, *History of the American Frontier*
1926—Edward Channing, *History of the United States,* Vol. VI.
1927—Samuel Flagg Bemis, *Pinckney's Treaty*
1928—Vernon Louis Parrington, *Main Currents in American Thought*
1929—Fred A. Shannon, *The Organization and Administration of the Union Army, 1861-65*
1930—Claude H. Van Tyne, *The War of Independence*
1931—Bernadotte E. Schmitt, *The Coming of the War, 1914*
1932—General John J. Pershing, *My Experiences in the World War*

1933—Frederick Jackson Turner, *The Significance of Sections in American History*
1934—Herbert Agar, *The People's Choice*
1935—Charles McLean Andrews, *The Colonial Period of American History*
1936—Andrew C. McLaughlin, *A Constitutional History of the United States*
1937—Van Wyck Brooks, *The Flowering of New England*
1938—Paul Herman Buck, *The Road to Reunion*
1939—Frank Luther Mott, *A History of American Magazines*
1940—Carl Sandburg, *Abraham Lincoln: The War Years*
1941—Marcus Lee Hansen (posthumous), *The Atlantic Migration*
1942—Margaret Leech, *Reveille in Washington*
1943—Esther Forbes, *Paul Revere and the World He Lived In*
1944—Merle Curti, *The Growth of American Thought*
1945—Stephen Bonsal, *Unfinished Business*
1946—Arthur Schlesinger, Jr., *The Age of Jackson*
1947—Dr. James Phinney Baxter III, *Scientists Against Time*
1948—Bernard De Voto, *Across the Wide Missouri*
1949—Roy F. Nichols, *The Disruption of American Democracy*
1950—O. W. Larkin, *Art and Life in America*
1951—R. Carlyle Buley, *The Old Northwest, Pioneer Period, 1815-1840*
1952—Oscar Handlin, *The Uprooted*
1953—George Dangerfield, *The Era of Good Feelings*
1954—Bruce Catton, *A Stillness at Appomattox*
1955—Paul Horgan, *Great River: The Rio Grande in North American History*
1956—Richard Hofstadter, *The Age of Reform*
1957—George F. Kennan, *Russia Leaves the War*
1958—Bray Hammond, *Banks and Politics in America—From the Revolution to the Civil War*

1959—Leonard D. White, *The Republican Era, 1869-1901*
1960—Margaret Leech, *In the Days of McKinley*
1961—Herbert Feis, *Between War and Peace: The Potsdam Conference*
1962—Lawrence H. Gipson, *The Triumphant Empire, Thunder Clouds Gather in the West*
1963—Constance McLaughlin Green, *Washington, Village and Capital 1800-1878*
1964—Sumner Chilton Powell, *Puritan Village: The Formation of a New England Town*
1965—Irwin Unger, *Greenback Era*
1966—Perry Miller (*post obitum*), *The Life of the Mind in America: From the Revolution to the Civil War*

*General Non-fiction*

1962—Theodore White, *The Making of the President, 1960*
1963—Barbara Tuchman, *The Guns of August*
1964—Richard Hofstadter, *Anti-Intellectualism in American Life*
1965—Howard Mumford Jones, *O Strange New World*
1966—Edwin Way Teale, *Wandering Through Winter*

*Drama*

1918—Jesse Lynch Williams, *Why Marry?*
1919—No award
1920—Eugene O'Neill, *Beyond the Horizon*
1921—Zona Gale, *Miss Lulu Bett*
1922—Eugene O'Neill, *Anna Christie*
1923—Owen Davis, *Icebound*
1924—Hatcher Hughes, *Hell-Bent for Heaven*
1925—Sidney Howard, *They Knew What They Wanted*
1926—George Kelly, *Craig's Wife*
1927—Paul Green, *In Abraham's Bosom*
1928—Eugene O'Neill, *Strange Interlude*
1929—Elmer Rice, *Street Scene*
1930—Marc Connelly, *The Green Pastures*

1931—Susan Glaspell, *Alison's House*
1932—George S. Kaufman, Morrie Ryskind, and Ira Gershwin, *Of Thee I Sing*
1933—Maxwell Anderson, *Both Your Houses*
1934—Sidney Kingsley, *Men in White*
1935—Zoë Akins, *The Old Maid*
1936—Robert E. Sherwood, *Idiot's Delight*
1937—George S. Kaufman and Moss Hart, *You Can't Take It with You*
1938—Thornton Wilder, *Our Town*
1939—Robert E. Sherwood, *Abe Lincoln in Illinois*
1940—William Saroyan, *The Time of Your Life* (declined)
1941—Robert E. Sherwood, *There Shall Be No Night*
1942—No award
1943—Thornton Wilder, *The Skin of Our Teeth*
1944—No award
1945—Mary Chase, *Harvey*
1946—Howard Lindsay and Russel Crouse, *State of the Union*
1947—No award
1948—Tennessee Williams, *A Street Car Named Desire*
1949—Arthur Miller, *Death of a Salesman*
1950—Richard Rodgers, Oscar Hammerstein II, and Joshua Logan, *South Pacific*
1951—No award
1952—Joseph Kramm, *The Shrike*
1953—William Inge, *Picnic*
1954—John Patrick, *Teahouse of the August Moon*
1955—Tennessee Williams, *Cat on a Hot Tin Roof*
1956—Frances Goodrich and Albert Hackett, *The Diary of Anne Frank*
1957—Eugene O'Neill, *Long Day's Journey Into Night*
1958—Ketti Frings, *Look Homeward, Angel*
1959—Archibald MacLeish, *J. B.*
1960—George Abbott, Jerome Weidman, Sheldon Harnick and Jerry Bock, *Fiorello*
1961—Tad Mosel, *All the Way Home*

1962—Frank Loesser and Abe Burrows, *How to Succeed in Business without Really Trying*
1963—No award
1964—No award
1965—Frank Gilroy, *The Subject Was Roses*
1966—No award

*The National Book Awards*

The National Book Awards are presented annually for books which five panels of judges consider the most distinguished books written by American citizens and published in the United States in the preceding year.

*Fiction*

1950—Nelson Algren, *The Man with the Golden Arm*
1951—William Faulkner, *Collected Stories*
Special Citation to Brendan Gill, *The Trouble of One House*
1952—James Jones, *From Here to Eternity*
1953—Ralph Ellison, *Invisible Man*
1954—Saul Bellow, *The Adventures of Augie March*
1955—William Faulkner, *A Fable*
1956—John O'Hara, *Ten North Frederick*
1957—Wright Morris, *The Field of Vision*
1958—John Cheever, *The Wapshot Chronicle*
1959—Bernard Malamud, *The Magic Barrel*
1960—Philip Roth, *Goodbye, Columbus*
1961—Conrad Richter, *The Waters of Kronos*
1962—Walker Percy, *The Moviegoer*
1963—J. F. Powers, *Morte D'Urban*
1964—John Updike, *The Centaur*
1965—Saul Bellow, *Herzog*
1966—Katherine Anne Porter, *Collected Stories*

*Poetry*

1950—William Carlos Williams, *Paterson III* and *Selected Poems*

1951—Wallace Stevens, *The Auroras of Autumn*
1952—Marianne Moore, *Collected Poems*
1953—Archibald MacLeish, *Collected Poems, 1917-1952*
1954—Conrad Aiken, *Collected Poems*
1955—Wallace Stevens, *The Collected Poems of Wallace Stevens*
Special citation to E. E. Cummings, *Poems: 1923-1954*
1956—W. H. Auden, *The Shield of Achilles*
1957—Richard Wilbur, *Things of This World*
1958—Robert Penn Warren, *Promises: Poems 1954-1956*
1959—Theodore Roethke, *Words for the Wind*
1960—Robert Lowell, *Life Studies*
1961—Randall Jarrell, *The Woman at the Washington Zoo*
1962—Alan Dugan, *Poems*
1963—William Stafford, *Traveling Through the Dark*
1964—John Crowe Ransom, *Selected Poems*
1965—Theodore Roethke (posthumous), *The Far Field*
1966—James Dickey, *Buckdancer's Choice*

*Non-Fiction*

1950—Ralph L. Rusk, *Ralph Waldo Emerson*
1951—Newton Arvin, *Herman Melville*
1952—Rachel Carson, *The Sea Around Us*
1953—Bernard DeVoto, *The Course of Empire*
1954—Bruce Catton, *A Stillness at Appomattox*
1955—Joseph Wood Krutch, *The Measure of Man*
1956—Herbert Kubly, *American in Italy*
1957—George F. Kennan, *Russia Leaves the War*
1958—Catherine Drinker Bowen, *The Lion and the Throne*
1959—J. Christopher Herold, *Mistress to an Age*
1960—Richard Ellman, *James Joyce*
1961—William L. Shirer, *The Rise and Fall of the Third Reich*
1962—Lewis Mumford, *The City in History*
1963—Leon Edel, *Henry James: The Conquest of London; Henry James: The Middle Years*

1964—*Arts and Letters:* Aileen Ward, *John Keats: The Making of a Poet*
*History and Biography:* William H. McNeill, *The Rise of the West*
*Science, Philosophy, and Religion:* Christopher Tunnard and Boris Pushkarev, *Man-Made America: Chaos or Control?*

1965—*Arts and Letters:* Eleanor Clark, *The Oysters of Locmariaquer*
*History and Biography:* Louis Fischer, *The Life of Lenin*
*Science, Philosophy, and Religion:* Norbert Wiener (posthumous), *God and Golem, Inc.*

1966—*Arts and Letters:* Janet Flanner (Genêt), *Paris Journal (1944-1965)*
*History and Biography:* Arthur M. Schlesinger, Jr., *A Thousand Days*

*Newbery Medal Awards*

The John Newbery Medal is awarded annually for the most distinguished contribution to literature for American children.

| | Title | Author |
|---|---|---|
| 1922 | *Story of Mankind* | Hendrik van Loon |
| 1923 | *Voyages of Dr. Dolittle* | Hugh Lofting |
| 1924 | *Dark Frigate* | Charles B. Hawes |
| 1925 | *Tales from Silver Lands* | Charles J. Finger |
| 1926 | *Shen of the Sea* | Arthur B. Chrisman |
| 1927 | *Smoky, the Cowhorse* | Will James |
| 1928 | *Gay-Neck* | Dhan Gopal Mukerji |
| 1929 | *Trumpeter of Krakow* | Eric P. Kelly |
| 1930 | *Hitty* | Rachel Field |

| | | |
|---|---|---|
| 1931 | *The Cat Who Went to Heaven* | Elizabeth J. Coatsworth |
| 1932 | *Waterless Mountain* | Laura Armer |
| 1933 | *Young Fu of the Upper Yangtze* | Elizabeth F. Lewis |
| 1934 | *Invincible Louisa* | Cornelia Meigs |
| 1935 | *Dobry* | Monica Shannon |
| 1936 | *Caddie Woodlawn* | Carol R. Brink |
| 1937 | *Roller Skates* | Ruth Sawyer |
| 1938 | *White Stag* | Kate Seredy |
| 1939 | *Thimble Summer* | Elizabeth Enright |
| 1940 | *Daniel Boone* | James Daugherty |
| 1941 | *Call It Courage* | Armstrong Sperry |
| 1942 | *Matchlock Gun* | Walter D. Edmonds |
| 1943 | *Adam of the Road* | Elizabeth Janet Gray |
| 1944 | *Johnny Tremain* | Esther Forbes |
| 1945 | *Rabbit Hill* | Robert Lawson |
| 1946 | *Strawberry Girl* | Lois Lenski |
| 1947 | *Miss Hickory* | Carolyn Sherwin Bailey |
| 1948 | *Twenty-One Balloons* | William Pène du Bois |
| 1949 | *King of the Wind* | Marguerite Henry |
| 1950 | *Door in the Wall* | Marguerite de Angeli |
| 1951 | *Amos Fortune, Free Man* | Elizabeth Yates |
| 1952 | *Ginger Pye* | Eleanor Estes |
| 1953 | *Secret of the Andes* | Ann Nolan Clark |
| 1954 | *. . . And Now Miguel* | Joseph Krumgold |
| 1955 | *Wheel on the School* | Meindert DeJong |
| 1956 | *Carry On, Mr. Bowditch* | Jean Lee Latham |
| 1957 | *Miracles on Maple Hill* | Virginia Sorensen |
| 1958 | *Rifles for Watie* | Harold Keith |
| 1959 | *Witch of Blackbird Pond* | Elizabeth George Speare |

| | | |
|---|---|---|
| 1960 | *Onion John* | Joseph Krumgold |
| 1961 | *Island of the Blue Dolphins* | Scott O'Dell |
| 1962 | *The Bronze Bow* | Elizabeth George Speare |
| 1963 | *Wrinkle in Time* | Madelene L'Engle |
| 1964 | *It's Like This, Cat* | Emily Neville |
| 1965 | *Shadow of a Bull* | Maia Wojciechowska |
| 1966 | *I, Juan de Pareja* | Elizabeth Borton de Trevino |

*Caldecott Medal Awards*

The Caldecott Medal is awarded to the illustrator of the most distinguished American picture book for children.

| | Title | Author and Illustrator |
|---|---|---|
| 1938 | *Animals of the Bible* | Dorothy Lathrop |
| 1939 | *Mei Li* | Thomas Handforth |
| 1940 | *Abraham Lincoln* | Ingri and Edgar d'Aulaire |
| 1941 | *They Were Strong and Good* | Robert Lawson |
| 1942 | *Make Way for Duck-lings* | Robert McCloskey |
| 1943 | *Little House* | Virginia Burton |
| 1944 | *Many Moons* | James Thurber and Louis Slobodkin |
| 1945 | *Prayer for a Child* | Rachel Field and Elizabeth Orton Jones |
| 1946 | *Rooster Crows* | Maud and Miska Petersham |
| 1947 | *The Little Island* | Golden MacDonald and Leonard Weisgard |
| 1948 | *White Snow, Bright Snow* | Alvin Tresselt and Roger Duvoisin |
| 1949 | *The Big Snow* | Berta and Elmer Hader |
| 1950 | *Song of the Swallows* | Leo Politi |
| 1951 | *The Egg Tree* | Katherine Milhous |
| 1952 | *Finders Keepers* | Will and Nicolas |
| 1953 | *Biggest Bear* | Lynd Ward |

| | | |
|---|---|---|
| 1954 | *Madeline's Rescue* | Ludwig Bemelmans |
| 1955 | *Cinderella* | Marcia Brown |
| 1956 | *A Frog Went A'Courtin'* | John Langstaff and Feodor Rojankovsky |
| 1957 | *A Tree Is Nice* | Janice May Udry and Marc Simont |
| 1958 | *Time of Wonder* | Robert McCloskey |
| 1959 | *Chanticleer and the Fox* | Barbara Cooney |
| 1960 | *Nine Days to Christmas* | Marie Hall Ets and Aurora Labistida |
| 1961 | *Baboushka and the Three Kings* | Ruth Robbins and Nicolas Sidjakov |
| 1962 | *Once a Mouse* | Marcia Brown |
| 1963 | *The Snowy Day* | Ezra Jack Keats |
| 1964 | *Where the Wild Things Are* | Maurice Sendak |
| 1965 | *May I Bring a Friend?* | Beatrice de Regniers and Beni Montresor |
| 1966 | *Always Room for One More* | Sorche Nic Leodhas and Nonny Hogrogian |

## *The Use of Quotations in Book Reviews*

Book reviewers often want to include in their reviews quotations from the books they are discussing. The following statements from the copyright pages of books or the printed review slips of various book publishers will help reviewers to decide how much may be quoted. Note that although each of these statements has been issued by a different publisher, essentially they are in agreement.

> Please feel free to quote up to 500 words. If you would like to use longer portions, we hope you will check with us for special permission.

No part of this book may be reproduced in any form without permission in writing from the publisher, except by a reviewer who wishes to quote brief passages in connection with a review written for inclusion in a magazine, newspaper or broadcast.

No part of this book may be reproduced in any form (including educational television), except by a reviewer, without the permission of the publisher.

Special permission is required to quote more than 500 words. No dramatization in lectures, television, or radio is allowed.

Direct quotation in reviews is limited to 500 words unless special permission is given.

No part of this book may be used or reproduced in any manner whatsoever without written permission except in the case of brief quotations embodied in critical articles and reviews.